TIMOTHY D. KANOLD
Series Editor

W9-CEH-090

COMMON CORE
Mathematics
in a PLC at Work™

LEADER'S GUIDE

Timothy D. Kanold
Matthew R. Larson
FOREWORD BY Douglas B. Reeves

A Joint Publication With

NCTM

NATIONAL COUNCIL OF
TEACHERS OF MATHEMATICS

555 North Morton Street
Bloomington, IN 47404

800.733.6786 (toll free) / 812.336.7700
FAX: 812.336.7790

email: info@solution-tree.com
solution-tree.com

Visit **go.solution-tree.com/commoncore** to download the reproducibles in this book.

Printed in the United States of America

16 15 14 13 12   2 3 4 5

Library of Congress Cataloging-in-Publication Data

Kanold, Timothy D.
   Common core mathematics in a PLC at work. Leader's guide / Timothy D. Kanold, Matthew R. Larson; Timothy D. Kanold, series editor ; foreword, Douglas B. Reeves.
      p. cm.
   Includes bibliographical references and index.
   ISBN 978-1-936765-47-8 (perfect bound : alk. paper) -- ISBN 978-1-936765-48-5 (library ed. : alk. paper) 1. Mathematics--Study and teaching--Standards--United States. 2. Educational leadership. 3. Professional learning communities. I. Larson, Matthew R. II. Title.
   QA13.K356 2012
   510.71'073--dc23
                                    2012014049

Solution Tree
Jeffrey C. Jones, CEO
Edward M. Ackerman, President

Solution Tree Press
President: Douglas M. Rife
Publisher: Robert D. Clouse
Vice President of Production: Gretchen Knapp
Managing Production Editor: Caroline Wise
Senior Production Editor: Joan Irwin
Copy Editor: Sarah Payne-Mills
Proofreader: Michelle Cohen
Text Designer: Amy Shock
Cover Designer: Jenn Taylor

Acknowledgments

To Tammy, who supports my being gone from home way more than I have a right to expect. Thank you to all the dedicated math instructional coaches in Lincoln (past and present) who make much of my work possible: Delise Andrews, Darla Berks, Sue Graupner, Kristin Johnson, Susie Katt, Julie Kreizel, Amy Nebesniak, Laura Parn, and Jerel Welker.

Thank you to all the mathematics education leaders who have taken the time to mentor and support my work: Mary Connolly, Chuck Friesen, Ruth Heaton, Mary Jacobsen, Jim Lewis, Cathy Seeley, Lee Stiff, and Bruce Vogeli.

Finally, a special thank-you to Tim Kanold. This series would not be possible without Tim's vision, commitment to the profession, and indefatigably positive attitude. But most of all, thank you for being my mentor and friend.

—Matthew R. Larson

My heartfelt thanks to Matt for his dedicated, creative, and tireless effort to turn the idea of this book into a collaborative reality.

Special thanks to Solution Tree—Jeff, Douglas, Gretchen, Joan, and Sarah—for their time, tireless effort, commitment, and belief in the importance of this work for the mathematics community.

Sincere thanks to the National Council of Teachers of Mathematics and the Educational Materials Committee for their support of this series and their leadership in the mathematics education of teachers and students.

Thanks to all of the authors and reviewers for this series. Many of their great ideas surface across the books and serve to bring coherence to the Common Core mathematics message.

Finally, this book and this series required a commitment of time that could not have been possible without the remarkable and enduring support of my wife, Susan, and our children—Jessica, a middle school mathematics teacher and principal; Adam, a civil engineer, who actually uses his college- and career-readiness mathematics skills; and Anna, who as a high school junior is a recipient of this national movement for improvement.

Susan, thank you for being a constant sounding board of reason to my many ideas for improvement and change, pushing me to write and edit this series, and keeping me grounded in the reality of my work.

—Timothy D. Kanold

Solution Tree Press would like to thank the following reviewers:

William Barnes
Coordinator of Secondary Mathematics
Howard County Public School System
Ellicott City, Maryland

Dianne DeMille
Cofounder
Global-Educational-Technologies, Inc.
Fullerton, California

Donna Simpson Leak
Superintendent
Rich Township High School
    District 227
Olympia Fields, Illinois

Steven Leinwand
Principal Research Analyst
American Institutes for Research
Washington, DC

Randy Pippen
Founder and Mathematics Consultant
Pippen Consulting
Treasurer
National Council of Supervisors of
    Mathematics
Plainfield, Illinois

Dan Galloway
Lead Consultant
Common Core PLC Learning Group
Former Principal
Adlai E. Stevenson High School District
    125
Phoenix, Arizona

Visit **go.solution-tree.com/commoncore** to download the
reproducibles in this book.

Table of Contents

About the Series Editor

Timothy D. Kanold, PhD, is a mathematics educator, author, and consultant. He is former director of mathematics and science and superintendent of Adlai E. Stevenson High School District 125, a model professional learning community district in Lincolnshire, Illinois.

Dr. Kanold is committed to equity and excellence for students, faculty, and school administrators. He conducts highly motivational professional development leadership seminars worldwide with a focus on turning school vision into realized action that creates greater equity for students through the effective delivery of professional learning communities for faculty and administrators.

He is a past president of the National Council of Supervisors of Mathematics and coauthor of several best-selling mathematics textbooks over several decades. He has served on writing commissions for the National Council of Teachers of Mathematics. He has authored numerous articles and chapters on school mathematics, leadership, and development for education publications.

In 2010, Dr. Kanold received the prestigious international Damen Award for outstanding contributions to the leadership field of education from Loyola University Chicago. He also received the Outstanding Administrator Award from the Illinois State Board of Education in 1994 and the Presidential Award for Excellence in Mathematics and Science Teaching in 1986. He now serves as an adjunct faculty member for the graduate school at Loyola University Chicago.

Dr. Kanold earned a bachelor's degree in education and a master's degree in mathematics from Illinois State University. He completed a master's in educational administration at the University of Illinois and received a doctorate in educational leadership and counseling psychology from Loyola University Chicago.

To learn more about Dr. Kanold's work, visit his blog Turning Vision Into Action at http://tkanold.blogspot.com, or follow @tkanold on Twitter.

To book Dr. Kanold for professional development, contact pd@solution-tree.com.

About the Authors

Matthew R. Larson, PhD, is a school district administrator, author, and nationally known speaker. He is the K–12 curriculum specialist for mathematics for Lincoln Public Schools, in Lincoln, Nebraska, where part of his work focuses on implementing effective professional learning communities to improve mathematics instruction and student achievement.

Dr. Larson has taught mathematics at elementary through college levels and has held an honorary appointment as a visiting associate professor of mathematics education at Teachers College, Columbia University. He is the coauthor of several elementary mathematics textbooks, professional books, and articles in mathematics education publications.

He is a member of the Board of Directors for the National Council of Teachers of Mathematics and has served on a variety of NCTM committees and task forces. Dr. Larson is a frequent and popular presenter at national and regional mathematics conferences, and his presentations are well known for their application of research findings to practice.

He earned his bachelor's degree and doctorate from the University of Nebraska–Lincoln.

To book Dr. Larson for professional development, contact pd@solution-tree.com.

In addition to being the series editor, **Timothy D. Kanold**, PhD, is a coauthor on this book.

Foreword

Math teachers can be an ornery lot. I should know, as I am one. We have seen scores of initiatives come and go, each implying that our previous practices have been woefully misdirected and that if only we had the insights and wisdom of the latest fad, we could restore student performance and regain our professional competence. Therefore, if math teachers are sometimes seen as the leading skeptics of the faculty, we have good reason for this reputation. What we would like, as Aretha Franklin famously said, is a little respect. Kanold and Larson deliver not only respect for teachers but also practical guidelines for the harried classroom professional, along with abundant evidence to satisfy the skeptic. This book is a gift to the profession, and it comes precisely when we need it. As you contemplate the pages that follow, I would like to advance four arguments to set the context for the work that lies ahead.

First, mathematics is not merely an academic issue but one of citizenship. While the Common Core State Standards and their associated assessments provide the current impetus for paying attention to the mathematical skills of students, the biggest question, rather than how students perform on a test, is how they exercise their rights as citizens in a democracy that depends on critical thinking. When politicians use charts, graphs, averages, and other representations of data to argue a point, our students must be prepared to ask probing questions that challenge prevailing wisdom. Our future physicians, mechanics, therapists, entrepreneurs, and teachers, along with those who will work in fields we cannot even contemplate, will require mathematical reasoning to succeed. Our students must confront profoundly complex issues ranging from national budget deficits to underfunded pension liabilities to personal and family financial planning, all of which necessitate mathematical skills and critical thinking. Our job is not to develop students who merely know the right answers but rather to develop citizens who ask the right questions.

Second, the teaching of mathematics must become more collaborative. Kanold and Larson identify seven distinct phases of teacher collaboration, and we ignore this nuanced process at our peril. Collaboration does not occur with an administratively mandated meeting or with the application of the phrase *professional learning community* to relabel previous practices. Genuine collaboration requires conversation, reflection, adaption, experimentation, and personal accountability for results. This imperative for teacher-to-teacher collaboration is particularly true in the discipline of mathematics, where faculty members almost always have greater subject matter expertise than school and district administrators. Our monopoly on expertise is a double-edged sword. We can genuinely value teacher leadership, creating a model for the entire school community. On the other hand, it is too easy to fake collaboration when we are the only people in the faculty meeting who can do recreational calculus. Expertise carries a serious responsibility to our peers and, most of all, to our students. If we accept that mathematics is about more than passing tests and developing short-lived and little-used formulae—that it is about developing critical-thinking skills that must be used in every class, not just for school but for a lifetime—then we bear a heavy responsibility for the care with which we nurture and improve our best teaching practices.

Third, excellence in the teaching and learning of mathematics depends on great leadership from the classroom to the boardroom. This does not mean that every school administrator, superintendent, and board member must attain mathematical expertise. It does, however, require administrative and policy leaders to allocate time and resources for classrooms, as well as for teachers in mathematics and other disciplines to conduct active inquiries about the impact of their teaching on student performance. Leaders must understand that excellence in mathematics instruction is not about "delivery," where, at the end of a lecture, everyone knows that the teacher is the smartest person in the room, or at the very least, the person in the room most acquainted with the textbook. Rather, excellence depends on a continuous cycle of challenge, inquiry, analysis, experimentation, feedback, and reflection. Leaders do not need to understand multivariate analysis, but they do need to understand that teaching, like life, is multivariate. Teaching and learning are complex endeavors, and the multiple variables include student background, home language, prior knowledge, opportunity to practice, willingness to ask for assistance, and a host of other social, cultural, and educational factors. Leaders who only exhort teachers to have *higher* scores are no more helpful than those who make excuses for low performance based on the demographic characteristics of their students. The best instructional leaders will help all teachers by ensuring they have access to data as well as the time and opportunity to analyze the data, test new instructional hypotheses, and reflect on the results.

Fourth, students will watch what we do in the classroom, comparing our actions to our claims. Students' critical-reasoning skills are rarely more finely honed than when applied to parents and teachers. Students will have little regard for what we say or for the words that district, state, or national documents contain. Thus, Kanold and Larson wisely focus on the daily activities of classroom teachers. Assessments, feedback, homework, and grading systems are the real stuff of which student-teacher interactions are made. While I endorse the Common Core State Standards, the greatest flaw in those documents is the claim that we can divorce the *what* of teaching from the *how* of daily practice. As the authors of this book suggest, the content of the Common Core and successful teaching methods are inseparable.

Perhaps the most notable feature of this book is not merely the competence of the content but the underlying spirit of commitment to equity that pervades every page. The authors understand that we cannot outsource mathematical proficiency as we have outsourced manufacturing; to do so would be to outsource our responsibility as educators and as citizens. Their most inspiring guidance confronts the issue every teacher has faced: What do we do when students don't get it? How do we respond to failure? In too many schools, the response to failure in mathematics has been the acquiescence to failure, leading to the resegregation of schools to a level not seen since Brown v. Board of Education. Crudely put, even in schools that pride themselves on a commitment to social justice and equity, white kids take calculus and statistics, and minority kids take remedial math. It is no different than if they had attended schools on opposite sides of the tracks half a century ago. If we are to confront this challenge, then we must heed the counsel that Tim Kanold and Matt Larson offer. Our response to failure cannot be a continuation of divergent opportunities based on student background but rather must be a commitment to equity that will prepare our students to think critically and lead boldly.

—Douglas B. Reeves

Introduction

These Standards are not intended to be new names for old ways of doing business. They are a call to take the next step. It is time for states to work together to build on lessons learned from two decades of standards based reforms. It is time to recognize that standards are not just promises to our children, but promises we intend to keep.

—National Governors Association Center for Best Practices &
Council of Chief State School Officers (NGA & CCSSO)

One of the greatest equity considerations with mathematics instruction, and instruction in general in most school districts, is that it is too inconsistent from classroom to classroom, school to school, and district to district (Morris & Hiebert, 2011). How much mathematics a fourth-, eighth-, or tenth-grade student in the United States learns, and how deeply he or she learns it, is largely determined by the school the student attends and, even more significantly, the teacher the student is randomly (usually) assigned to within that school. The inconsistencies teachers develop in their professional development practice—often random and in isolation from other teachers—create great inequities in students' mathematics instructional and assessment learning experiences that ultimately and significantly contribute to the year-by-year achievement gap (Ferrini-Mundy, Graham, Johnson, & Mills, 1998). This issue is especially true in a vertically connected curriculum like mathematics and is likely familiar based on your own experiences as well.

The hope and the promise of the *Common Core Mathematics in a PLC at Work*™ series is to provide the guidance and leadership focus for the teacher professional development needed to work outside of existing paradigms regarding mathematics teaching, assessing, and learning. The resources in this leader's guide for the series will enable you to focus your time and energy on issues and actions that will lead to ensuring your faculty and staff address the Common Core State Standards (CCSS) for mathematics challenge: *All students successfully learning rigorous standards for college or career-preparatory mathematics.*

Most of what you will read and use in this book, as well as this series, has been part of the national discussion on mathematics reform and improvement since the National Council of Teachers of Mathematics' (NCTM) release of the *Curriculum and Evaluation Standards for School Mathematics* in June of 1989. In 2000, NCTM refocused the nation's vision for K–12 mathematics teaching, learning, and assessing in *Principles and Standards for School Mathematics* (PSSM). The National Research Council (NRC) followed by providing supportive research in the groundbreaking book *Adding It Up*

(NRC, 2001). Visit **go.solution-tree.com/commoncore** for a more detailed history of mathematics standards development.

So, what would cause you as an educational or mathematics leader to believe the national, state, and local responses to the CCSS for mathematics will be any different this time than previous reform efforts and recommendations?

Your leadership. Your ability to help your faculty and staff focus on the right things—the things that will actually enhance student learning. Your leadership must communicate the specific steps you and your school or district will take to move from a culture focused on covering mathematics curriculum to a culture fixated on each student's learning, from a culture of teacher isolation to a culture of purposeful collaboration and collective responsibility, from a culture where assessment is used as a tool to prove what students have or have not learned to a culture where assessment is used to *improve* on student learning, from a culture where evidence of student learning is used primarily to assign grades to a culture where evidence of student learning is used to inform and improve professional practice, student focus, and action.

The full implementation of the previous mathematics teaching and learning frameworks and standards was limited by the very system of the previous states' standards mathematics *assessments*. Although the standards might have been rigorous, the assessment of those standards was not. This caused local district resistance to teaching the deeper, richer mathematics curriculum recommended in the CCSS. This resistance was primarily due to state testing that reflected only the lower-cognitive, procedural knowledge aspects of the states' standards. In many school districts, it often felt like a race to get through the grade-level or course curriculum before April of each school year as the *wytiwyg* phenomenon—what you test is what you get—kicked in.

The Education Trust (Ushomirsky & Hall, 2010) in *Stuck Schools: A Framework for Identifying Schools Where Students Need Change—Now!* indicates that in an environment in which funds and capacity are limited at best, educators and policymakers will need to establish clear priorities. The five paradigms for action described in *Common Core Mathematics in a PLC at Work, Leader's Guide* establish those priorities and will provide the basis for your day-to-day decision making. These paradigms are built on a foundation of equity, collegial relations, student-engaged learning, effective unit-by-unit planning and design, assessment as a motivational student tool, and the provision of adequate time and support to achieve these goals.

In many cases, this series recommends priorities that will require a paradigm shift in fundamental *beliefs and behaviors* about mathematics teaching and learning by you and your faculty. The CCSS expectations for teaching and learning and the new state assessments of that learning usher in an opportunity for unprecedented *second-order change*. *First-order change* is characterized as working within existing paradigms with marginal disturbance to the system and implemented within the existing knowledge and skill set of those closest to the action—the faculty and school leaders. Second-order change requires working outside the existing system by embracing new paradigms for how you think and practice (Waters, Marzano, & McNulty, 2003). Until now, there has been a lot of debate but no clear turning point with respect to K–12 mathematics education improvement. The standards themselves won't impact student achievement. However, the CCSS for mathematics represent a collective and collaborative statewide effort to signal that turning point. The CCSS will be your catalyst for providing the support you need as a leader to effect real change.

This book is for a broadly defined base of school leaders—including superintendents, assistant superintendents for curriculum or instruction, principals, assistant principals, teacher leaders, instructional specialists and coaches, department chairs, district and county mathematics coordinators, and college and university mathematics program leaders. The series focuses on five fundamental leadership areas necessary to help you prepare every teacher for the successful implementation of the CCSS for mathematics, ultimately leading to the general improvement of teaching and learning for all students. These areas provide the framework within which second-order change can be successfully achieved. The five critical areas are the following.

1. **Collaboration:** The CCSS require a shift in the *grain size of change* beyond the individual isolated teacher or leader. It is the grade-level or course-based collaborative learning team (collaborative team) within a Professional Learning Community (PLC) at Work culture that will develop the expanded teacher knowledge capacity necessary to bring coherence to the implementation of the CCSS for mathematics. The grain size of change now lies within the power and voice of collaborative teams in your PLC. Your leadership role is to provide the conditions, structures, and culture necessary to eradicate the old paradigm of isolated teacher decision making and the inequities in student learning caused by such practice. Leading and designing high-performing collaborative teams in mathematics is described in chapter 1.

2. **Instruction:** The CCSS require a shift to daily lesson designs that include plans to engage students in the Mathematical Practices that focus on the process of learning and developing deep understanding of the content standards. This change requires teaching for student understanding of the grade-level CCSS content *and* teaching for procedural fluency. One should not exist without the other. This will require your instructional support for helping faculty and staff commit to the use of student-engaged learning around common high-cognitive-demand mathematical tasks used in every classroom. Leading this paradigm for an effective vision of mathematics instruction is described in chapter 2.

3. **Content:** The CCSS require a shift to *less* (fewer standards) is *more* (deeper rigor with understanding) at each grade level. This change will require new levels of knowledge and skill development for every teacher of mathematics to understand *what* the CCSS expect students to learn at each grade level or in each course blended with *how* they expect students to learn it. What are the mathematical knowledge, skills, understandings, and dispositions that should be the result of each unit of mathematics instruction? A school and mathematics

program committed to helping all students learn ensures great clarity and low teacher-to-teacher variance on the questions, What should students learn? How should they learn it? Your role is to ensure that the correct unit-by-unit collaborative team planning for the correct content and the progressions of that content are aligned and targeted toward the rigor and expectations of the CCSS. Chapter 3 describes your leadership role in supporting the content paradigm.

4. **Assessment:** The CCSS require a shift to assessments that are a *means* within the teaching-assessing-learning cycle and not used as an *end* to the cycle. These assessments must reflect the rigor of the standards and model the expectations for and benefits of formative assessment practices around all forms of assessment, including traditional assessment instruments such as tests and quizzes. *How will teachers and teacher teams know* if each student is learning the essential mathematics skills, concepts, understandings, and dispositions the CCSS deem most essential? *How will teachers and teacher teams know* if their students are prepared for the more rigorous state assessment consortia expectations from the Partnership for Assessment of Readiness for College and Careers (PARCC) and the SMARTER Balanced Assessment Consortium (SBAC)? The primary goal of each organization is to create high-quality assessments that provide a mix of items—short answer, open response, performance based, and multiple choice— that reflect the complete range of skills and content in CCSS mathematics. *How will you help* every teacher to build proficiency in the use of formative assessment practices that meet the expectations of assessment within the Common Core? You must have a crystal-clear vision for the ongoing mathematics assessment you are willing to support in your school or district. Chapter 4 describes developing your formative assessment vision, understanding the role equity plays in that vision, and using tools to obtain that vision.

5. **Intervention:** The CCSS require a shift in your teacher team and overall school response to intervention (RTI). RTI can no longer be invitational. That is, the response to intervention becomes R^2TI—a required response to intervention. Stakeholder implementation of RTI programs includes a process that *requires* students to participate and attend. How will you *respond* and act on evidence (or lack of evidence) of student learning in your school or district? It is critical that you remove any barriers to having a systemic and team-level response to intervention. A PLC leader responds immediately and with great clarity when students fail to learn. Chapter 5 describes how to do so.

The intent of this book and this series is to support your CCSS mathematics leadership work and to focus the work, time, and effort of your mathematics programs and collaborative teams on high-impact actions for improving student learning.

Each chapter of the book explores how to lead these five intricately woven paradigm shifts—second-order changes necessary to improve your mathematics program and attain student achievement. First, as you do your work *together* and strive to achieve the PLC culture through your well-designed grade-level or vertical collaborative teams, teacher knowledge capacity will only grow and flourish if led well. Each chapter's Extending My Understanding section has resources and tools you can use in collaborative teams to make sense of and reflect on the chapter recommendations. Second, as a leader of effective collaborative teams (grade level or course based), you can make *great decisions* about teaching, learning, assessing, and how your response to learning will impact student mathematics achievement. As Jim Collins and Morten T. Hansen (2011) indicate in *Great by Choice*, you may not be able to predict the future, but you and your collaborative teams can create it. Your professional development goal should be to help every teacher and teacher leader make great decisions toward a great mathematics future for students—every day.

CHAPTER 1

Leading High-Performing Collaborative Teams for Mathematics

The Common Core State Standards provide a consistent, clear understanding of what students are expected to learn, so that teachers and parents know what they need to do to help them learn. The standards are designed to be robust and relevant to the real world, reflecting the knowledge and skills that our young people need for success in college and careers. With American students fully prepared for the future, our communities will be best positioned to compete successfully in the global economy.

—NGA & CCSSO

The mission of the K–12 CCSS for mathematics is ambitious yet attainable. Thus, it will require your strong leadership for the right kind of professional development—professional development that leads to effective and consistently implemented instructional and assessment practices. To successfully and equitably implement these expectations, the teachers you lead must be engaged in an ongoing *process* of professional development and learning. Among your primary leadership responsibilities are to monitor, pressure, and support the successful implementation of the CCSS for mathematics—at your level of leadership and influence within the school organization.

For this to happen, you will need to establish and lead a coherent and ongoing professional development *process* that supplies every teacher with the confidence and pedagogical knowledge capacity necessary to improve his or her mathematics teaching, assessment methods, and ability to take action and support students to take action on mathematics assessment results.

The Professional Development Paradigm Shift

One of the primary characteristics of high-performing and high-impact schools—schools that are successfully closing the mathematics achievement gap—is their laserlike focus on teacher collaboration as a key to improving instruction and reaching all students (Education Trust, 2005; Kersaint, 2007). Traditional professional development that relies on one-shot workshop models outside of teachers' work environment and nurtures an expectation of teacher isolation without support or pressure for implementation does not result in significant improvements in student achievement. The professional development of teachers and leaders can no longer rely on singular events or isolated trainings as is typical in the old paradigm.

For professional development and learning to become effective, an ongoing, continuous, sustainable, and collaborative activity inside the school is needed. Research on effective professional development programs—those that provide between thirty and one hundred hours of contact time with teachers over the course of six to twelve months—demonstrates a positive, significant, and sustained effect on student achievement (Wei, Darling-Hammond, Andree, Richardson, & Orphanos, 2009).

Strong effects for professional development on teacher practice occur when the professional development is focused on enhancing teachers' knowledge of how to engage in specific pedagogical skills and how to teach specific kinds of content in order to enhance student learning (Blank, de las Alas, & Smith, 2007). The most effective professional development immerses teachers in collaboratively studying, in a structured way, the very curriculum they will teach, as well as their students' acquisition of that curriculum—down to the lesson level. This approach ultimately leads more teachers to adopt the curricular and instructional innovations from the school district's instructional vision (Huggins, Scheurich, & Morgan, 2011; Penuel, Fishman, Yamaguchi, & Gallagher, 2007; Wayne, Kwang, Zhu, Cronen, & Garet, 2008).

Teacher participation in collaborative team discussions *removes several barriers* to the creation and implementation of a rigorous and coherent mathematics curriculum. Implementing the CCSS for mathematics means individual members of your collaborative teams can no longer afford to take weeks out of each school year to reteach content, crowd the curriculum with favorite projects, fail to challenge students to think mathematically, or deliver instruction that is ineffective. Working with colleagues, each teacher on a collaborative team begins to "balance personal goals with collective goals, acquire resources for his or her own work, and share those resources to support the work of others" (Garmston & Wellman, 2009, p. 33). As Kanold (2011a) explains:

> This is the wonderful paradox of the loose-tight or "defined autonomy" PLC culture. Adults can work within a defined set of behaviors [the CCSS expectations] and have an opportunity for freedom and choice. . . . Autonomy is different from independence. Autonomy in the loose-tight PLC world does not mean the individualistic going it alone, relying on nobody. Yet, rather as Daniel Pink (2009) points out, autonomy means "acting with choice—which means we can be both autonomous and happily interdependent with others." (p. 48)

The issue for you as a school leader is not about protecting individual teacher autonomy. Rather, the issue lies in your ability to teach and support collaborative team autonomy and transparency using the research-based tools necessary to collaboratively reflect and experiment in ways that are connected to the vision and mission of your school district to improve student learning.

As a school leader, you influence this subtle yet important shift toward using collaborative professional development time for rigorous thinking, execution, and capacity building of the faculty and staff. The paradigm shift: *professional development is no longer an event that occurs occasionally in a teacher's and leader's life*; professional development with other colleagues becomes the teacher's and leader's way of life. This new paradigm for professional development envisions mathematics teachers and other specialists collaborating interdependently to deepen their knowledge of mathematics pedagogical content and competencies, and expects *action on that knowledge* with application to practice. Part of your role as a school leader is to ensure teacher action on that knowledge.

Given the high stakes of increased academic achievement for all students, teacher collaboration with peers must be *nondiscretionary*. Mathematics teachers in your school cannot opt out of working with peers when it comes to issues related to student learning. The act of becoming an effective teacher can no longer be about *my* students or *your* students. It is about *our* students and what each teacher and leader can do to benefit *all* students in a grade level or course. Teachers in your school or district who opt to work in isolation miss the chance to learn from others, and they fail to fully understand the benefits and the responsibility of being interdependent colleagues. When teachers collaborate on mathematics teaching and learning, they grow as effective mathematics teachers. That growth is a never-ending aspect of a teacher's professional journey, and it is your leadership challenge and responsibility to help that journey be an enjoyable and meaningful experience for each teacher in your school or district.

Collaborative grade-level or course-based learning teams become the engines for change in your school or district. Building the knowledge capacity of the collaborative learning team, and focusing that capacity on student learning, are primary responsibilities of your leadership work and influence. This is best done through well-designed communities of practice—*professional learning communities* (Schmoker, 2005).

Professional Learning Communities: Your Vehicle for Professional Development

Not surprisingly, many school leaders, teachers, and administrators equate professional learning communities with teacher collaboration. As such, *PLC* is a term that is fairly ubiquitous in education. At the same time, various definitions and understandings regarding a PLC *culture* abound. In this book, DuFour, DuFour, and Eaker's (2008) *Revisiting Professional Learning Communities at Work* and DuFour, DuFour, Eaker, and Many's (2010) *Learning by Doing* are used to define the conditions for collaborative mathematics learning teams in an authentic PLC culture. For our purposes, we refer to grade-level or course-based groups of teachers and leaders working together in a PLC as *collaborative teams*.

Just as students in groups need direction and support from the teacher to work well together, teachers and other educational stakeholders in collaborative teams need direction and support from you, as a school leader, to learn how to *collaborate* well and move beyond low-level team conversations.

The collective CCSS mathematics teamwork of PLCs focuses on designing practice around four fundamental agreements (DuFour et al., 2008). These four agreements are:

1. What students should learn—clarifying the essential student learning clusters and outcomes—including *how* students learn the *what* through engagement with the CCSS Mathematical Practices learning processes (chapters 2 and 3)

2. The development and use of common and coherent assessments to determine if students have learned the agreed-on curriculum—*how* will you know if students are learning? (chapters 2 and 4)

3. How to collectively respond in class and out of class when students don't learn the agreed-on curriculum of the CCSS (chapters 4 and 5)

4. How to collectively respond in class and out of class when students do learn the agreed-on curriculum of the CCSS (chapters 4 and 5)

In order for collaborative mathematics teams to respond to these four professional learning community agreements, you must provide the time, access, support, and accountability for the teams to do their work.

American educators often speak to a shared vision, but that vision is not usually fine-tuned to address the specific work needs of the collaborative teams in your school. Thus, teachers often work toward success for every student without a coordinated image of what that might look like in the classroom. Similar to providing students with a target to aim toward, collaborative teams need a shared vision of curriculum, instruction, assessment, and intervention that is specific to learning mathematics. As Danielson (2009) argues, "It's not sufficient for a school to be comprised of individual expertise; that expertise must be mobilized in the service of a common vision" (p. 17). For example, if you surveyed a random selection of ten teachers in your school, would they all be able to describe the same mathematics instructional vision for their grade level or course? Is the vision for instruction crystal clear and coherent for them?

Thus, a shared vision is a necessary cornerstone to the work of your collaborative teams. Your teams might already have a shared vision in place, which is a good start. Yet it is not sufficient. Teacher team inquiry, action orientation, experimentation, and reflection enable you to make progress toward the vision with fidelity of purpose. In many schools, teachers are working in teams and using data to set goals and monitor progress. Does this describe the work of collaborative teams at your school? If so, it is also an important and necessary action, but again, not sufficient.

Although given less attention, the difficult collaborative teamwork of collective inquiry, together with action orientation and experimentation, has a more direct impact on student learning than teachers working in isolation (Hattie, 2009). It is in the process of inquiry and experimentation that team members find meaning in collaborative work with others. It is through the respectful challenging of their peers about what does and does not work in the classroom that teachers take ownership of their own beliefs, learning, and professional development. In the collective creation, modification, and ongoing reflection of what is taught and how instruction impacts student learning, teachers begin to pursue personal growth as professionals.

Teacher collaboration is about *purposeful peer interaction* (Fullan, 2008). If PLC team collaboration is to influence and impact teacher learning, then teachers, teacher leaders, and administrators become intentional about the nature and content of the collaboration.

The collaboration of your teams must be purposeful and focused. According to Reeves (2010), high-impact professional development and learning in collaborative teams:

1. Focus on student learning

2. Focus on assessment of the decisions teacher team members make

3. Attend to people and practices rather than programs

In this sense, members of your collaborative teams collect and analyze data to determine if their instructional decisions (their behaviors and practices) had an impact on student learning. In this scenario, you attend to the needs of the teachers in your sphere of leadership by creating and supporting collaborative work that pushes teacher peers to critically examine student learning. As teachers collectively analyze student work, classroom practices, and dialogue about mathematical content, the impact on student achievement is far greater than discussions about predesigned lessons to teach. The PLC teaching-assessing-learning cycle described in chapter 4 is designed to support this type of meaningful collaborative team inquiry and work.

Collaboration is not necessarily efficient or easy. However, when teachers have the skills and knowledge to collaborate through professional conversations focused on student learning, the dialogue, reflection, and actions emerge as a form of ongoing professional learning and teacher development. As Fullan (2008) indicates, collaborative learning is your work. Leading others in collaborative learning begins by recognizing the different stages that lead to authentic teacher team collaboration and helping your teams move through those stages.

Teacher Collaboration Versus Cooperation or Coordination

There is a caution for you as you examine the level of actual or authentic collaboration of your various teacher teams. What is often considered teacher *collaboration* is actually cooperation or coordination. *Cooperation* is an informal process for sharing information with no goal or outcome in mind (Grover, 1996). Cooperation is about being a *team player*. One potential danger of cooperation is the exclusion of team members' diverse ideas. Consider a scenario in which your team members share ideas and lesson plans about how they each teach a learning target about triangles in a geometry unit. In this case, teachers cooperate by sharing resources, although each teacher retains his or her own authority to teach and assess the learning targets.

Coordination on the other hand requires more teacher team planning and communication than cooperation. Efficiency regarding the management aspects of a given unit of instruction tends to drive teachers to coordinate. For example, a Third-Grade Team or a High School Geometry Team may coordinate a schedule so all teachers have access to modeling materials for the unit, or they might divide up different standards from a CCSS content standard cluster in order to design lessons. Note that coordination can serve purposes of efficiency but does little to push *inquiry and discussion of the daily instruction and assessment in the classroom*—the true purpose and high-leverage work of PLC collaborative teams.

Whereas *cooperating* and *coordinating* are about *individuals* on the teacher team making decisions, *collaboration* is about creating interdependence with colleagues as they work beyond consensus building. When your teams are effectively collaborating, you will observe team members creating new structures and ways of working that are focused on academic success for all students, not just the students in their own classes. Your leadership role is to monitor the teacher team meeting and observe the type of work and discussions taking place and to provide formative guidance about how to deepen the quality of the team's work.

To support your team-monitoring effort, Graham and Ferriter (2008) offer a useful diagnostic tool framework that details seven stages of teacher collaboration. You can use this framework as a diagnostic check to determine the level of authentic collaboration currently taking place in the teams you lead. Table 1.1 highlights an adapted version of the seven stages.

Table 1.1: Seven Stages of Teacher Collaboration

Stage	Questions That Define This Stage
Stage one: Filling the time	What exactly are we supposed to do as a team?
Stage two: Sharing personal practice	What is everyone doing in his or her classroom for instruction, lesson planning, and assessment?
Stage three: Planning, planning, planning	What should we be teaching during this unit, and how do we lighten the load for each other?
Stage four: Developing common assessments	How will we know if students learned the standards? What does mastery look like for the standards in this unit?
Stage five: Analyzing student learning	Are students learning what they are supposed to be learning? Do we agree on student evidence of learning?
Stage six: Adapting instruction to student needs	How can we adjust instruction to help those students struggling and those exceeding expectations?
Stage seven: Reflecting on instruction	Which lesson-design practices are most effective with our students?

Visit **go.solution-tree.com/commoncore** for a reproducible version of this table.

Teams that are at the first three stages of collaborative team development are trying to understand what they are supposed to do and accomplish as a team. They may need your help in setting their agendas, bringing a focus to their work, and learning how to plan for the unit-by-unit work of the team—calendars, assignments, projects, timing of review days, and so on. Teams in stages four and five are coordinating common planning of instruction and assessment, developing common assessment instruments and tasks, and analyzing student results. The teams may not take collective action on those results, but they are coordinating the generation and use of common learning targets, mathematical tasks, and assessments. It is in the final two stages that teams are actually *collaborating* as members take collective responsibility for the learning of all students, differentiating instruction based on their collective understanding of student progress and designing assessments based on student needs by reflecting on the question, "Which practices are most effective with our students?" (Graham & Ferriter, 2008, p. 42). If, after analyzing the data from the unit common assessment instrument (test), your teams develop a differentiated lesson design to either extend the knowledge and reasoning of students who have mastered the learning target or to provide targeted support for struggling learners (stage six), then a more authentic and interdependent collaboration is under way. Collaborative teams achieve stage seven when they regularly make adjustments to instruction based on learner needs and discuss and implement instructional and assessment strategies that have the greatest impact on student learning.

You can use table 1.1 to help your teams diagnose, monitor, and assess their collaborative teams' stages of development and supply crucial data to the professional development action required for their growth as collaborative teams. You should use this tool to measure the stage at which each team in your sphere of influence operates. Are they cooperating, coordinating, or collaborating? When the teams in your PLC work together, you can observe to determine: Are discussions focused on sharing lessons or activities without inquiry into assessing student learning? Are meetings centered on when the unit test will be given in class without questioning how teachers are connecting larger concepts throughout the unit? You can use the table 1.1 descriptors to determine the current stage of team development throughout your school and to help your teams become more aware of whether or not their weekly meetings and discussions are moving beyond cooperation and into the desired direction of stage six and stage seven collaboration. However, there are several barriers to effective collaboration that you can help remove to ensure your collaborative teams are maximizing their potential.

Leading Collaborative Practices

One of the goals of stage seven is to pursue high *within-school* teacher knowledge capacity and low *between-teacher* implementation variance in terms of mathematics content, pedagogical knowledge, and assessment knowledge. According to Barber and Mourshed (2007) in *How the World's Best Performing School Systems Come Out on Top*, the world's highest-performing school systems are able to "decrease the pedagogical variability between teachers and increase the quality of instruction. . . . They do this by establishing clear instructional priorities and investing in teacher preparation and professional development" (p. 12). Five critical collaborative team areas impact effectiveness and will need your support. They are:

1. Participation

2. Commitments

3. Leaders

4. Agendas and meeting minutes

5. Team time

In order to do the teamwork described in figure 1.1 and to move effectively and efficiently to the more advanced stages of team collaboration, it is important you provide guidance to your teams for each of these five collaboration factors.

Participation

The members of the various collaborative teams under your influence will vary according to the needs of your school or district. For larger schools, collaborative teams may be comprised of all teachers of a particular course, content level, or grade level. For example, a collaborative team may be all teachers of advanced algebra or mathematics 2, teachers of multiple grade levels (like seventh or eighth grade), teachers of a single grade level (like all third-grade teachers), or those who teach honors-level mathematics courses. Your collaborative teams also benefit from other faculty and staff members participating on the team. School support personnel such as counselors, special needs or English learner (EL) teachers, or paraprofessional tutors might also be considered to participate on various mathematics collaborative teams, as they can both receive and provide insight and support to a coherent collaborative team response to intervention in your school or district.

For smaller schools, your teams might be too small. It can be difficult to collaborate when there are a limited number of teachers in your school or there is only one grade-level or course-based teacher. In that case, the collaborative team can expand to include all members of a grade band, like 3–5, or all members of a department. *Personal learning networks* (PLNs)—groups of colleagues and experts that communicate, usually in an online capacity, to learn and share information—also greatly enhance teachers' collaboration. Teachers can share information with colleagues (a *blog buddy* perhaps) outside of their school. Their work together might focus more on vertical articulation, sharing of expectations for learning targets, common unit-by-unit tasks, assessments, and the effective instruction and support needed for all students.

Team members need only have a common curricular, instructional, or assessment focus about which to collaborate. While there is no ideal or magic number of teachers on a collaborative team, experience seems to suggest that teams much larger than seven or eight can be challenging. When your teams are too large, discussions become unwieldy, and a few extroverted teachers can hijack participation, limiting the voices of other team members who may not be heard (Horn, 2010). It is possible for larger teams to engage in productive dialogue. However, a higher level of facilitation of the collaborative work will be required to ensure all voices are heard. Principals, mathematics department chairs, or K–12 instructional leaders and coaches should also consider teacher compatibility and social/emotional intelligence when determining teacher assignments each year (Goleman, 2007).

Commitments

You, as a school leader, need to explicitly communicate expectations for how collaboration looks and sounds. In *What Works in Schools*, Marzano (2003) identifies the necessity for collegiality. *Collegiality* is defined as the way teachers interact with each other in a manner that is professional. Roland Barth (2006) provides a description of collegiality.

> When I visit a school and look for evidence of collegiality among teachers and administrators—signs that educators are "playing together"—the indicators I seek are:
>
> 1. Educators talking with one another about practice
> 2. Educators sharing their craft knowledge
> 3. Educators observing one another while they are engaged in practice
> 4. Educators rooting for one another's success (p. 10)

Michael Fullan and Andy Hargreaves (1996) explain that professional behaviors include respect for one another, a willingness to share mistakes, and an openness to critique practices and procedures (as cited in Marzano, 2003). Sharing mistakes and being open to criticism can be daunting. Thus, your teams will need to establish and enforce norms or collective commitments of conduct and behavior if teachers are to work in collaborative teams that promote a level of openness and vulnerability.

The purpose of designing collective team commitments is to create a respectful, open environment that encourages diversity of ideas and invites professional criticism combined with close inspection of practices and procedures. Various protocols are available to assist your teams in establishing actions to which team members agree to adhere. The process need not be arduous, complicated, or time consuming. The protocol in figure 1.1 is one model you can use to establish and then review your collaborative teams' collective commitments throughout the year.

Setting Team Collective Commitments

Because we need our best from one another when working as a team, it is essential that we set collective commitments for our work cultures. Collective commitments are values and beliefs that will describe how we choose to treat each other and how we can expect to be treated.

As we set three to four collective commitments for ourselves, please note that establishing these does not mean that we are not already good people who work together productively. Having collective commitments simply reminds us to be highly conscious about our actions and what we can expect from each other as we engage in conversations about our challenging work.

Step One

Write three or four "We will" statements that you think will have the most positive influence on our group as we collaborate on significant issues about teaching and learning. Perhaps reflect on past actions or behaviors that have made teams less than productive. These are only a jumpstart for your thinking.

Step Two

Partner with another colleague to talk about your choices and the reasons for your selection. Together decide on three or four commitments from your combined lists.

Figure 1.1: Setting teacher team collective commitments protocol. continued →

Step Three

Partner with two or four other colleagues to talk about your choices and the reasons for your selection. Together decide on three or four commitments from your combined lists.

Step Four

Make a group decision. Prepare to share your choices with the whole group.

Step Five

Adopt collective commitments by consensus. Invite clarification and advocacy for particular commitments. Give all participants four votes for norm selection. It is wise not to have more than five or six norms.

Source: Adapted from P. Luidens, personal communication, January 27 and April 9, 2010.

Visit **go.solution-tree.com/commoncore** for a reproducible version of this figure.

Your collaborative teams should keep collective commitments focused on behaviors and practices that will support your team's collaborative work. Some teams find it useful to post their norms in a conspicuous place as a reminder to each other. Other collaborative teams might choose a commitment to highlight at each meeting as a reminder of their commitments. (Visit www.allthingsplc.info under Tools & Resources for additional ideas.)

For one particular mathematics collaborative team, members decided to make their collective commitments to (1) listen to understand others, (2) challenge ideas respectfully, and (3) keep the agenda focused on teaching and learning. Although the team was relatively the same group as the previous year, members reflected on the previous year and felt that sometimes one or two individuals passionate about their ideas often hijacked the discussions without hearing others' ideas. The collective commitments reflect the collaborative team's dedication to hearing all ideas and respectfully challenging each other.

Your leadership can help each team member take responsibility to hold one another accountable for the agreed-on team commitments. This is a form of peer-to-peer, or *lateral*, accountability. It must become a permissible and expected aspect of the team culture for team members to address those members not adhering to the norms. If needed, you must help your collaborative teams establish a process that addresses what happens when team norms are not honored. The purpose of the collective commitments and norms is to raise the level of professionalism and liberate the team to openly, safely, and respectfully discuss the work at hand.

Your leadership role is to help each team develop a clear conflict-resolution plan, should members violate the norms. Kanold (2011a) provides one such process team members could follow—Care Enough to Confront, which requires team members to keep a short account of any issue. As he describes:

> Every team encounters some adversity as members debate and argue about important practices and methods for the teaching and learning. Once the *care enough to confront* discussion is completed, everyone on the team must let it go, move on, and keep a short mental account of the

issue. Team members who harbor long-term resentments will be toxic to the team's growth. (p. 109)

As collaborative teams grow, develop, or change membership, collective commitments and ways to celebrate and be accountable to those commitments will likely change. Regardless of whether the collaborative team commitments do change, each year collective commitments should be revisited and reviewed. This will be more beneficial if done at the start of the year and at the end of each semester.

Leaders

Just as effective staff development needs planning and facilitation, collaborative team meetings also need intentional forethought and a team leader. The role of team leader or meeting facilitator might rotate or be delegated to one individual. On one hand, one person assigned team leader for the entire school year might bring continuity to team discussions and functions. (A team leader may have other responsibilities related to the team's work in addition to leading team meetings.) On the other hand, rotating the role of team leader or meeting facilitator gives more teachers the opportunity to take ownership and develop in their ability to facilitate discussions.

To make the most of the collaborative team meeting time, an effective collaborative team always knows who is *driving the meeting bus*. The team leader should be an intentional choice on your part, so as to maximize the team's ability to collaborate by inviting diversity of thought and challenging ideas and practices. An effective team leader will encourage all members to participate and ask questions to push for clarity and understanding. An effective team leader will also summarize team questions, understandings, decisions, and actionable items as he or she collaborates with you to help achieve the broader goals of the school. This person provides the follow-up work for team action.

One of your responsibilities is to provide ongoing training for your team leaders to make sure they are confident to manage the energy and the pacing of the meetings and ensure the meeting is effective for all participants, including members who do not process information as quickly as others.

Agendas and Meeting Minutes

Designing collaborative teams for mathematics is a considerable commitment of resources in people, money, and time. The payoff occurs when the teacher collaboration around teaching and learning mathematics results in professional growth and increased student achievement. Agendas and minutes of each meeting are tools that lend themselves to more efficient use of time. The designated team leader takes responsibility for seeking input from team members, determining the agenda, and making the agenda public to you and the team a few days prior to the meeting. Agendas acknowledge that time is valuable. They are essential to successful meetings (Garmston & Wellman, 2009). An agenda need not be complicated or long, but it needs to be purposeful. You should monitor the team agendas, and they should be posted electronically for review. Figure 1.2 (page 18) provides a sample mathematics agenda from a seventh-grade collaborative team.

Tuesday, October 16

- Share and analyze results from exponents unit assessment.
  - How did our students do overall?
  - Were the results what we expected?
  - Did anyone's students do better on each learning standard? What might those teachers have done differently than the rest of us?
- Review learning targets for the statistics unit.
  - Do our learning targets capture the key content concepts?
  - Do the learning targets together represent a balance of higher-level reasoning and procedural fluencies?
- Bring ideas for introducing statistics.
  - What have you tried in the past that seems to have worked?
  - Are there ideas, problems, and strategies that you tried that didn't work?
  - What task or problem might we use to help understand our students' prior knowledge about statistics?

Figure 1.2: Sample team meeting agenda.

Visit **go.solution-tree.com/commoncore** for a reproducible version of this figure.

Notice that the agenda is composed of quick bullet points that communicate the focus of the meeting so your team members can come prepared with ideas, data, or other possible resources. Also note that the team leader provides guiding questions for team members to reflect on prior to the meeting. The team leader has primed the pump of the meeting expectations, so to speak. If the team leader does not know how to do this, you may need to give him or her guidance until he or she is confident in this peer leadership role. Team members who give prior thought and consideration to the agenda topics make the meeting more productive.

Meeting minutes, similar to the agenda, are beneficial, should be posted electronically, and do not need to be overly detailed. Minutes serve many useful purposes. First, minutes for each meeting capture the actions and decisions that the team has made. Teams have found it useful to go back to minutes from earlier in the year or even from the previous year to recall discussions related to the ordering of content or why they decided to use a particular instructional approach for a concept. Minutes also capture who is responsible for various action steps, such as creating a scoring rubric and key for a quiz or test or arranging artifact copies for all team members. The minutes provide you with quick insight into the activities of the team.

Second, the team meeting minutes are an efficient way to communicate to others what transpired at the meeting. If a teacher is unable to attend a meeting, you can use the minutes as a resource to let him or her know what the team discussed and decided. Much like students absent from class, teachers absent from a team meeting are still expected to know and carry out the team's decisions (and you must make this expectation clear to them). Technology is an effective means by which to make minutes public to others. Minutes can be posted in email, or to a wiki, a blog, or a team website, to name a few.

Finally, the minutes provide you with targeted guidance, direction, or resources to support your collaborative team's work. Figure 1.3 provides an example of a High School Geometry Team's meeting minutes that were electronically posted.

- After today's meeting, we are thinking about doing a variation of Val's social-emotional learning activity after the first quiz, which we'll discuss at the next meeting.

- We discussed how to deal with the shortened first-term grading period. We are thinking we should stay with the plan of giving the cumulative exam on the Monday after the grading period ends.

- We discussed ways to deal with properties of quadrilaterals rather than doing the lab. We decided to eliminate the lab because it does not mirror the student problem-solving thought process we are trying to develop for this unit.

- We decided on partial credit for multiple-choice questions on tests and the formulas to use in chapter 12, as long as students show all work.

Figure 1.3: Sample Geometry Team meeting minutes.

Visit **go.solution-tree.com/commoncore** for a reproducible version of this figure.

Laying the groundwork for collaboration by articulating expectations of how collaborative teams will work together (toward constructive discussions and decision making) and the logistics of announcing and capturing your team discussions is essential. Attention to these fundamental team-management issues supports deeper and more meaningful discussions that will impact student mathematics learning. Once you have established, articulated, and enforced expectations about collaboration, your teams can engage in meaningful discussions around teaching and learning mathematics.

Team Time

Other than providing the right type of monitoring and guidance for teamwork, you should ensure teams have the necessary time to meet, which is one of the important aspects of your leadership role. Significant student achievement gains result when collaborative learning teams are provided with sufficient and consistent time to collaborate (Saunders, Goldenberg, & Gallimore, 2009). The world's highest-performing countries in mathematics or sustained educational improvers—Singapore, Hong Kong SAR, South Korea, Chinese Taipei, and Japan—allow significant time for mathematics teachers to collaborate and learn from one another (Stigler & Hiebert, 1999; Barber & Mourshed, 2007). Meaningful CCSS implementation will require time—time to digest the CCSS domains and content standard clusters, time to design lessons and tasks that engage students in the Mathematical Practice, time to create a coherent unit-by-unit curriculum implementation plan, time to design instruction and assessments together, and time to plan and deliver interventions as determined by students' learning needs.

Finding ways to make more effective use of the time currently available and seeking ways to enhance time available—*as part of the teachers' contractual workday*—are essential professional development issues for every school leader. Time is often the toughest challenge principals, school leaders, and teachers encounter. How can you find time for professional development activities in the already crowded school schedule?

Teaching children mathematics well is a complex activity that is learned through teacher knowledge sharing, coaching, professional development experiences, and field-based experience. Teachers as professionals need time to reflect on the success and failures of their daily lessons and weekly assessments with others who are working toward similar grade-level or course-based goals. By building time for professional development into the regular school day, you convey a message about the importance of continuous and ongoing learning. Although the grade-level books for the teachers and teacher teams in this series will provide more specific ideas for how to do so, insight into this process is available in "Making Time for Collaboration" at AllThingsPLC (n.d.; www.allthingsplc .info/pdf/articles/MakingTimeforCollaboration.pdf).

Figure 1.4 provides a few ideas for how to make collaborative team professional development time a priority in your school (Bowgren & Sever, 2010; Loucks-Horsley, Love, Stiles, Mundry, & Hewson, 2003).

---

1. Provide common time by scheduling most, if not all, team members to have the same period or time of day free from teaching.

2. Create an altered schedule for early-release or late-arrival students on an ongoing basis, if feasible to your community.

3. Use substitutes to roll through the day, releasing different collaborative teams for a few hours at a time.

4. Occasionally release teachers from teaching duties or other supervision duties in order to collaborate with colleagues.

5. Restructure time by permanently altering teacher responsibilities, the teaching schedule, the school day, or the school calendar.

6. Purchase teacher time by providing compensation for weekends and summer work.

Figure 1.4: Options for scheduling teacher collaboration time.

First and foremost, teachers need to be provided adequate time to achieve the expectations of ongoing weekly mathematics professional development. Reeves (2009) asserts it is a myth that people love to collaborate. He notes that real and meaningful collaboration requires time, practice, and accountability: "Schools that claim, for example, to be professional learning communities but fail to provide time for collaboration are engaging in self-delusion" (p. 46). School district leaders sincere in their efforts to create a PLC school culture will design creative ways to build time into the weekly schedule for collaboration around mathematics.

As teachers collaborate, their beliefs about teaching and learning are revealed. Through meaningful discourse, teams seek to reconcile inconsistency of ideas and practices in the quest to continuously improve student mathematics learning. This ongoing process of sharing, questioning, and reconciling ideas culminates in professional learning, which in turn brings about more equity and access for all students. As the school leader, you must ensure that each collaborative team is efficiently and effectively focused on activities and actions that have a high-leverage payoff for improving student achievement.

High-Leverage Professional Development for the Common Core

You can use figure 1.5 to help your collaborative teams focus their collective energy on meaningful collaboration activities on a unit-by-unit basis. This top-ten list provides a coherent focus for movement toward erasing current inequities in teacher practice and places teacher time and talent on actions that more directly impact student learning. In order to justify the time provided, quality teacher team collaboration should take place around high-leverage issues. Figure 1.5 provides specific guidance to the most essential issues for your teams' work. Each team's specific, measurable, attainable, results-oriented and time-bound (SMART) student achievement goal plan for the year should contain some elements of these ten essential team actions—depending on the focus of the team for the school year. You must help your teams to answer the question, How will we know if our work mattered?

Teaching and Learning

1. The team designs and implements agreed-on prior knowledge skills to be assessed and taught during each lesson of the unit. The collaborative teacher team reaches agreement for teaching and learning in the lessons and unit.

2. The team designs and implements agreed-on lesson-design elements that ensure active student engagement with the mathematics. Students experience some aspect of the CCSS Mathematical Practices, such as Construct viable arguments and critique the reasoning of others or Attend to precision, within the daily lessons of every unit or chapter.

3. The team designs and implements agreed-on lesson-design elements that allow for student-led summaries and demonstrations of learning the daily lesson.

4. The team designs and implements agreed-on lesson-design elements that include the strategic use of tools—including technology—for developing student understanding.

Assessment Instruments and Tools

1. The team designs and implements agreed-on common assessment instruments based on high-quality exam designs. The collaborative team designs all unit exams, unit quizzes, final exams, writing assignments, and projects for the course.

2. The team designs and implements agreed-on common assessment instrument scoring rubrics for each assessment in advance of the exam.

3. The team designs and implements agreed-on common scoring and grading feedback (level of specificity to the feedback) of the assessment instruments to students.

Figure 1.5: High-leverage unit-by-unit actions of mathematics collaborative teams.

continued →

Formative Assessment Feedback

1. The team designs and implements agreed-on adjustments to instruction and intentional student support based on both the results of daily formative classroom assessments and the results of student performance on unit or chapter assessment instruments such as quizzes and tests.

2. The team designs and implements agreed-on levels of rigor for daily in-class prompts and common high-cognitive-demand tasks used to assess student understanding of various mathematical concepts and skills. This also applies to variance in rigor and task selection for homework assignments and expectations for make-up work. This applies to depth, quality, and timeliness of teacher descriptive formative feedback on all student work.

3. The team designs and implements agreed-on methods to teach students to self-assess and set goals. Self-assessment includes students using teacher feedback, feedback from other students, or their own self-assessments to identify what they need to work on and to set goals for future learning.

Visit **go.solution-tree.com/commoncore** for a reproducible version of this figure.

Meaningful CCSS implementation will require time—time to digest the CCSS standards, content standard clusters, and Mathematical Practices; time to create a coherent curriculum; and time to design instruction and assessments around the high-leverage actions listed in figure 1.5. Use figure 1.5 as a monitoring tool as you examine the week-in, week-out work of your various collaborative teams.

Collaborative Protocols

Several protocols combine collaboration with a spotlight on the teaching and learning of mathematics. Five structured protocols can be especially beneficial in your work with diverse teacher teams. These protocols provide different settings in which you can collaborate and share reflections and beliefs about teaching and learning.

1. **Lesson study:** Lesson study differs from lesson planning. Lesson study focuses on what teachers want students to learn; lesson planning focuses on what teachers plan to teach. In lesson study, a teacher team develops a lesson together, and one teacher teaches the lesson while the others observe the student learning. (This part of the protocol will require your support with substitutes.) Each teacher collects observational data during the lesson to support the lesson's learning targets. The team then comes together to debrief the lesson and revise as needed to incorporate what students have learned.

   Lesson study may seem time and work intensive for a single lesson. Nonetheless, the benefit of lesson study is the teacher professional learning that results from the deep, collaborative discussions about mathematics content, instruction, and student learning. See the lesson-study references listed in the Extending My Understanding section (page 24) for more information about this powerful activity.

2. **Peer coaching:** Peer coaching is a kind of partnership in which two or three teachers engage in conversations focused on their reflections and thinking about their instructional practices. The discussions lead to a refinement and formative assessment response to classroom practice. The participants may rotate roles—discussion leader, mentor, or advocate. Teachers who engage in peer coaching are willing to reveal strengths and weaknesses to each other. Peer coaching creates an environment in which teachers can be secure, connected, and empowered through transparent discussions of each others' practice.

3. **Case study:** Case study can be used to address a wide range of topics or problems collaborative teams encounter. The case study presents a story—one involving issues or conflicts that need to be resolved through analysis of available resources leading to constructive plans to address the problem. Typically, case studies are used to examine complex problems—the school's culture, climate, attendance, achievement, teaching, and learning (Baccellieri, 2010). The best cases are based on team members' real classroom events. This is a great opportunity to expand the work of your coaches and instructional leaders to focus on the work of the team rather than individual teachers.

4. **Book study:** Book study is a familiar and popular activity for teachers to engage in conversations with colleagues about professional books. It may be a formalized activity for some collaborative teams; however, book study can emerge in any number of ways—from hearing an author speak at a conference, from a colleague's enthusiastic review of a book, or from the mutual interests of teachers who want to learn more about a topic. Book study promotes conversations among faculty and staff that can lead to the application of new ideas in the classroom and improvement of existing knowledge and skills. Book study is a great way to connect with a personal learning network as you blog, tweet, skype, or use other forms of communication to connect with colleagues outside of your school.

5. **Collaborative grading:** Collaborative grading occurs as your teams reach stages four and five (see table 1.1, page 12) of team collaboration. In this situation, you and your colleagues design a common unit test together and assign point values with scoring rubrics for each question on the exam. Teachers grade and discuss the quality of student responses on the assessment instrument together and develop an inter-rater reliability for scoring of the assessment tool. Achieving consistency in grading students' assignments and assessments is an important goal for collaborative teams.

From the point of view of instructional transparency and improvement, lesson study is a particularly powerful collaborative tool that merits close consideration. Lesson study has been shown to be very effective as a collaborative protocol with a high impact on teacher professional learning (Hiebert & Stigler, 1999).

Looking Ahead

Preparing to implement the CCSS provides a unique opportunity for your school or district to embrace the idea that schools should become learning institutions for the adults as well as the students. The CCSS in mathematics and in English language arts can serve as this catalyst. Effective professional development is not only a prerequisite for improved student achievement but also a commitment to the investment in the professionals who have the largest impact on students in schools.

The process of collaboration capitalizes on the fact that teachers come together to use diverse experiences and knowledge to create a whole that is larger than the sum of the parts. Teacher collaboration is *the* solution to sustained professional learning—an ongoing and never-ending process of teacher growth necessary to meet the demands of the CCSS expectations. The National Board for Professional Teaching Standards (2010) states the following with respect to professional teachers:

> Seeing themselves as partners with other teachers, they are dedicated to improving the profession. They care about the quality of teaching in their schools, and, to this end, their collaboration with colleagues is continuous and explicit. They recognize that collaborating in a professional learning community contributes to their own professional growth, as well as to the growth of their peers, for the benefit of student learning. Teachers promote the ideal that working collaboratively increases knowledge, reflection, and quality of practice and benefits the instructional program. (p. 75)

The new paradigm for the professional development of mathematics teachers requires an understanding that the knowledge capacity of every teacher matters. More importantly, however, is that every teacher *acts* on that knowledge and transfers the professional development he or she receives into daily classroom practice—truly closing the knowing-doing gap. Part of your leadership role is to ensure that every teacher grows professionally and subsequently acts on his or her new knowledge.

In the chapters that follow, the Standards for Mathematical Practice and the content standards of the CCSS will be unpacked, and the role collaborative teams play in implementing and supporting all students' successful acquisition of these new standards through highly effective instructional, assessment, and intervention practices will be explored in greater depth. We will provide tools to assist you in your work as you make the vision of the Common Core State Standards a reality in your school and for all students.

Chapter 1 Extending My Understanding

1. A critical tenet of a PLC's mathematics program is a shared vision for the teaching and learning mathematics in your school program.

    a. Do you have a shared vision of what teaching and learning mathematics looks like for your school or district? If not, how might you create one?

    b. Does this vision build on current research in mathematics education?

    c. Does your vision embrace collaboration as fundamental to the ongoing professional learning of faculty and staff?

2. Graham and Ferriter (2008) identify seven stages of collaborative team development. These stages characterize team development evolving from cooperating to coordinating, leading ultimately to a truly *collaborative* team.

   a. Using table 1.1 (page 12), at what stage are your various collaborative teams currently operating?

   b. What role might you play in helping your team transition toward stages six and seven?

3. Using figure 1.5 (page 21), identify the high-leverage actions your collaborative teams currently practice extremely well. Rate the current levels of implementation (0 percent low and 100 percent high). How might you use this information to identify which actions should be teams' priorities during this school year or the next school year?

4. Implementing the content and CCSS Mathematical Practices might seem daunting to some teachers, and as a result, there may be resistance to or half-hearted attempts at needed changes in content, instruction, or assessment. Consider leading your collaborative teams through a Best Hopes, Worst Fears activity. Give team members two index cards. On one, have them identify their best hopes for implementing the CCSS. On the other card, have team members record their worst fears. Depending on the level of trust and comfort of the team, you might collect the index cards and read the best hopes and worst fears anonymously, or individuals can read their hopes and fears aloud to the group. The purpose of this activity is to uncover concerns that if left undiscovered might undermine collaborative teamwork. Your teams should talk about how they can support one another to minimize fears and achieve best hopes.

5. Pages 22–23 list several collaborative protocols. Choose a protocol that you are either familiar with or would like to learn more about. How might you use that protocol to engage your various collaborative teams into a deeper discussion for implementing CCSS content or Mathematical Practices?

Online Resources

Visit **go.solution-tree.com/commoncore** for links to these resources. Visit **go.solution -tree.com/plcbooks** for additional resources about professional learning communities.

- *The Five Disciplines of PLC Leaders* (**Kanold, 2011a; go.solution-tree.com /plcbooks/Reproducibles_5DOPLCL.html**): Chapter 3 discusses the commitment to a shared mission and vision by all adults in a school for several tools targeted toward collaborative actions. These reproducibles engage teachers in professional learning and reflection.

- **Chicago Lesson Study Group** (**www.lessonstudygroup.net/index.php**): The Chicago Lesson Study Group provides a forum for teachers to learn about and practice lesson study as a way to steadily improve student learning. To learn more about lesson study or other collaborative protocols, the following resources are suggested.

- ○ *Lesson Study: A Handbook of Teacher-Led Instructional Change* (Lewis, 2002)
- ○ *Powerful Designs for Professional Learning* (Easton, 2008)
- ○ *Leading Lesson Study* (Stepanek, Appel, Leong, Managan, & Mitchell, 2007)
- ○ *Data-Driven Dialogue: A Facilitator's Guide to Collaborative Inquiry* (Wellman & Lipton, 2004)

- **AllThingsPLC (www.allthingsplc.info):** Search the Tools & Resources for sample agendas and activities for collaborative work.

- **The Center for Comprehensive School Reform and Improvement (www .centerforcsri.org/plc/websites.html):** The website offers a collection of resources to support an in-depth examination of the work of staff in learning teams.

- **Inside Mathematics (2010; www.insidemathematics.org/index.php /tools-for-teachers/tools-for-principals-and-administrators):** This portion of the Inside Mathematics website is designed to support school-based administrators and district mathematics supervisors who have the responsibility for establishing the structure and vision for the work of grade-level and cross-grade-level learning teams.

- **Learning Forward (2011; www.learningforward.org/standards/standards .cfm):** Learning Forward is an international association of learning educators focused on increasing student achievement through more effective professional learning. This website provides a wealth of resources, including an online annotated bibliography of articles and websites to support the work of professional learning teams.

- **The National Commission on Teaching and America's Future (Fulton & Britton, 2011; www.nctaf.org/wp-content/uploads/NCTAFreport STEMTeachersinPLCsFromGoodTeacherstoGreatTeaching.pdf):** With the support of the National Science Foundation and in collaboration with WestEd, NCTAF released *STEM Teachers in Professional Learning Communities: From Good Teachers to Great Teaching*. NCTAF and WestEd conducted a two-year analysis of research studies that document what happens when science, technology, engineering, and math teachers work together in professional learning communities to improve teaching and increase student achievement. This report summarizes that work and provides examples of projects building on that model.

- **The Mathematics Common Core Toolbox (www.ccsstoolbox.org):** This website provides coherent and research-affirmed protocols and tools to help you in your CCSS collaborative teamwork. The website also provides sample scope and sequence documents and advice for how to prepare for CCSS for mathematics implementation.

CHAPTER 2

Leading the Implementation of the Common Core Standards for Mathematical Practice

Reasoning and sense making must become a part of the fabric of the mathematics classroom. Not only are they important goals themselves, but they are the foundation for true mathematical competence. Incorporating isolated experiences with reasoning and sense making will not suffice. Teachers must consistently support and encourage students' progress toward more sophisticated levels of reasoning.

—NCTM

Mathematics education in the United States has a long history of confidence in standards and curriculum programs as the primary means to improve student achievement (Larson, 2009). However, reliance on standards and materials to improve student achievement has not resulted in dramatic improvements in student learning, and more importantly, it has not resulted in a narrowing of existing achievement gaps (Loveless, 2012). If CCSS *implementation* is to be more than a superficial gesture in your school or district—more than a content standards mapping—and is instead to result in real improvements in student learning and to close the achievement gap, then implementation efforts need to be more about instruction—*how* teachers approach student *learning* of the content standards. As Wiliam (2011) contends, "Pedagogy trumps curriculum. Or more precisely, pedagogy *is* curriculum, because what matters is how things are taught, rather than what is taught" (p. 13).

The CCSS for mathematics includes content standards for developing student *understanding* as well as standards for student proficiency in their mathematical *learning experiences.* In addition, "The Standards for Mathematical Practice describe varieties of expertise that mathematics educators at all levels should seek to develop in their students" (NGA & CCSSO, 2010, p. 6). (See appendix A, page 133.) When students are engaged in the Standards for Mathematical Practice, they are making and evaluating their conjectures as part of meaningful discussions with their peers.

The ultimate goal is to equip your students with expertise that will help them succeed in doing and using mathematics not only across the K–12 mathematics curriculum but also in their college and career work. College instructors rate the Mathematical Practices as being of higher value for students to master in order to succeed in their courses than any of the CCSS content standards. This was true for mathematics, language, science, and social sciences college instructors (Conley, Drummond, de Gonzalez, Rooseboom, & Stout, 2011). In this chapter, we examine the CCSS Mathematical Practices—what would you expect to observe in a classroom that embeds the Standards for Mathematical Practice in daily instruction? This chapter also examines lesson design and planning components, including a template for planning, which will support your current efforts to help teachers improve instruction and make the Mathematical Practices part of their daily planning. Finally, the chapter provides ideas for you to use with your collaborative teacher teams as they work together to make daily pedagogical decisions that create environments in which student demonstration of the Mathematical Practices is a key component of their instructional plans.

The CCSS for Mathematics Instructional Paradigm Shift

Research indicates that mathematics learning should go beyond demonstration of procedural content; it should include opportunities for students to reason and make sense of the mathematics they are learning. Specifically, the Standards for Mathematical Practice are built on NCTM's work (2000, 2006, 2009), in particular NCTM's emphasis on process standards in addition to content. Furthermore, the National Research Council (2001) defines mathematics learning and proficiency as consisting of much more than procedural knowledge. NCTM's and NRC's groundwork is reinforced and further refined in the CCSS Mathematical Practices.

As you support your collaborative teams' work to make sense of the Mathematical Practices, you should take advantage of this opportunity to develop a collective vision for effective and meaningful mathematics teaching. If your school or district has not already embarked on the journey of emphasizing student understanding, reasoning, problem solving, and sense making as part of your vision for instruction, now is the ideal time to help your collaborative teams abandon daily lessons devoid of mathematical reasoning and connected ideas and move to instruction that encourages students to think deeply about the mathematics content and demands them to understand and use it.

The consortia on performance-based assessment expectations of the Common Core mathematics will require you to ensure every teacher begins to embrace this instructional paradigm shift. Teaching only for procedural fluency is insufficient and fails to prepare students for the world they will live and work in after school. Developing students' deep understanding of content and using their conceptual understanding of mathematics as a precursor to developing procedural or symbolic fluency in mathematics is the new vision and paradigm for change. One cannot and should not exist without the other.

Do not wait one more unit, chapter, week, month, or year. This major change relies not so much on the vision for teaching mathematics, but on your leadership for turning that *vision into action*. The only way for you to answer whether or not a fundamental paradigm shift in mathematics instruction is needed in your school or district is to perform a teacher lesson-design and behavior check on current instructional practices throughout your school or district. This evaluation will require multiple observations in classrooms and discussions with the collaborative teams as you measure teacher instructional beliefs, vision, and action against the Standards for Mathematical Practice. Is there a gap between the expectations and beliefs for high-quality instruction and the actual implementation and action on those beliefs?

Boykin and Noguera (2011) point out that the direct teaching of and regular practice with the instructional strategies such as those expected in the CCSS Mathematical Practices (for example, ensuring opportunities for students to communicate, conjecture, and reason with peers) is rarely, if ever, done. They indicate "this state of pedagogical affairs needs to be rectified" (p. 125). Further, they state:

> Gap closing results did not occur in classrooms that primarily manifested "basic skills" instruction (ie: activities that require students to come up with yes or no responses that are either correct or incorrect). . . . One of the more actively researched areas for deep processing is referred to as cognitive elaboration. Here the focus is on going beyond "yes/no" or "true/false" answers, beyond bubbling in multiple-choice responses, and beyond providing simple names and dates for answers. Instead the focus is on enabling students to justify their answers, to provide more thoughtful and reflective answers, and to recognize their role as knowledge producers. (p. 126)

As you focus deliberate attention on implementing the CCSS Mathematical Practices, part of the challenge may be to envision what the practices look like in the classroom as part of instruction. The student tasks teachers design, the questions they ask to check for understanding in the classroom, and the discourse in which students participate will all combine to advance students' abilities to *engage* with peers in the Mathematical Practices. One way to begin and lead this process is to engage your collaborative teams in discussions around each of the eight CCSS Mathematical Practices as collaborative team members identify evidence of each practice in their daily and weekly lesson and unit designs.

The Common Core Standards for Mathematical Practice

As a school leader, and as someone who either supervises or evaluates instructional improvement, you have a role to communicate and monitor your expectations for daily instruction. Ultimately, it is your responsibility to ensure the vision for instruction becomes a reality in your school or district. The Standards for Mathematical Practice provide that vision.

The Standards for Mathematical Practice describe what students are *doing* as they engage in learning the Common Core mathematics content standards. How should students engage with mathematics tasks and interact with their fellow students? How well do teachers develop students' engagement in mathematics reflecting the CCSS Mathematical Practices? The Standards for Mathematical Practice are not a checklist of teacher to-dos, but rather they are *processes* and *proficiencies* for students to experience and demonstrate as they master the content standards. The eight Standards for Mathematical Practice each begin with the three words—*mathematically proficient students*. This language establishes an expectation for evidence of student growth toward proficiency in each of these eight practices as part of the K–12 mathematics learning experience.

As a result of your team discussions and efforts to modify instruction, you may be interested in tracking teachers' progress in implementing the Common Core mathematics and providing feedback. The Common Core Look-Fors Mathematics app (http://splaysoft.com/CCL4s/Welcome.html) for the iPad or iPhone is an example of one tool that tracks the growth of a teacher's transition through the implementation of the Common Core State Standards. This app provides suggested student actions for informal and formal peer observation and is a source for data analysis related to teaching. The app's *crowd-sourcing* feature allows users to access the online resources that other educators have shared, evaluated, and tagged to the Common Core content standards.

Figure 2.1 provides a framework for organizing the eight mathematical practices into four distinct student mathematical experiences regarding *how* students will engage in mathematics learning:

1. Overarching habits of mind

2. Reasoning and explaining

3. Modeling and using tools

4. Seeing structure and generalizing

Overarching Habits of Mind	Reasoning and Explaining
1. Make sense of problems and persevere in solving them. 6. Attend to precision.	2. Reason abstractly and quantitatively. 3. Construct viable arguments and critique the reasoning of others.
	Modeling and Using Tools
	4. Model with mathematics. 5. Use appropriate tools strategically.
	Seeing Structure and Generalizing
	7. Look for and make use of structure. 8. Look for and express regularity in repeated reasoning.

Figure 2.1: CCSS Mathematical Practices organization model.

There are two key questions you can use to help your collaborative teams develop understanding of the eight Standards for Mathematical Practice. See figure 2.2.

1. What is the intent of this CCSS Mathematical Practice?
2. How can the collaborative team address this CCSS Mathematical Practice?

Figure 2.2: Key questions used to understand the CCSS Mathematical Practices.

By first defining the Standard for Mathematical Practice through exposure of its meaning and examples, teachers working in course-based or grade-level learning teams can make sense of each Standard for Mathematical Practice, generate ideas for how to support the practice in daily lesson and weekly unit plans, and analyze ways to assess students' interactions using the CCSS Mathematical Practices.

Overarching Habits of Mind

When teaching mathematics, teachers often avoid planning for and using problem-solving tasks and activities that challenge students to persevere. According to results of the *TIMSS Videotape Classroom Study* (Stigler, Gonzales, Kawanka, Knoll, & Serrano, 1999), teachers' beliefs about teaching and learning often lead them to "design lessons that remove obstacles and minimize confusion [where] procedures for solving problems would be clearly demonstrated so students would not flounder or struggle" (p. 137). Lessons planned from this perspective, that students need protection from constructive struggle, do not support the perseverance aspects of Mathematical Practice 1—"Make sense of problems and persevere in solving them" and Mathematical Practice 6—"Attend to precision" and deny students the opportunity to develop meaningful mathematical understandings (Stein, Remillard, & Smith, 2007).

Mathematical Practice 1: Make Sense of Problems and Persevere in Solving Them

Mathematical Practice 1, Make sense of problems and persevere in solving them, refers to the ability of students to explain to themselves (and others) the meaning of a mathematical task or problem and look for entry points to its solution (NGA & CCSSO, 2010, p. 5).

What Is the Intent of Mathematical Practice 1?

Problem solving is one of the hallmarks of mathematics and is the essence of doing mathematics (NCTM, 1989). When students are engaged in problem solving, it means they are drawing on their understanding of mathematical concepts and procedures with the goal to reach a successful response to the problem.

As you study the expectations for Mathematical Practice 1, you will notice several areas for student proficiency including:

1. Students make conjectures about the meaning of a solution and plan a solution pathway.

2. Students try special cases or simpler forms to gain insight. (They hypothesize and test conjectures.)

3. Students monitor and evaluate their progress and discuss with others.

4. Students understand multiple approaches and ask the question, "Does this solution make sense?"

5. Students explain correspondence between equations, tables, graphs, verbal descriptions, and data, and they search for regularity, patterns, or trends.

Successful problem solving does not mean that students will always conclude with the correct response to a problem but rather that students will undertake a genuine effort to engage in the problem-solving process, drawing on learning resources described in the other practices such as appropriate tools, using their prior knowledge, engaging in mathematical discourse with other students, and asking questions to make progress in the problem-solving process. Successful problem solvers also recognize that powerful learning can be experienced even when an appropriate answer to a problem ultimately evades the student.

How Can the Collaborative Team Address Mathematical Practice 1?

Teachers play the important role in supporting students' ability to make sense of problems and persevere in solving them. The first of these roles is the presentation of appropriate problems or tasks for students to solve. While it seems that *appropriate* is subjective, figure 2.3 highlights six questions you can present to teachers for discussion within their collaborative teams when planning lessons to assess the quality of problem solving within a common or shared mathematical task.

As we develop common tasks and problems to be used during the unit, we should consider:

1. Is the problem interesting to students?

2. Does the problem involve meaningful mathematics?

3. Does the problem provide an opportunity for students to apply and extend mathematics?

4. Is the problem challenging for students?

5. Does the problem support the use of multiple strategies or solution pathways?

6. Will students' interactions with the problem and peers reveal information about their mathematics understanding?

Figure 2.3: Team planning questions that promote CCSS Mathematical Practice 1.

Visit **go.solution-tree.com/commoncore** for a reproducible version of this figure.

Observing students' interactions with a mathematical task (for example, students' work, discourse, tools, and representations) will provide information about how their thinking is hindered or evolving by interaction with the problem or task selected. This list of questions is not exhaustive, but it is a beginning step toward examining problems for the potential benefit they can provide for advancing students' mathematical problem solving and learning.

Your leadership role is to ensure collaborative teams discuss how to help students understand that the answer is not the final step in the problem-solving process. A great deal of mathematical learning can happen when students are guided to explain and justify processes and check the reasonableness or precision of the solution. After teaching lessons within the unit, teachers on the team should ask: "Is there evidence that students are learning other ways of solving the problem? Is there evidence that students are making and learning mathematical connections to other problems? Is there evidence students are making the effort to persevere when solving the problem?"

Mathematical Practice 6: Attend to Precision

Mathematical Practice 6, Attend to precision, refers to the need for students to communicate precisely and correctly (NGA & CCSSO, 2010, p. 7). This student proficiency is an important aspect of the learning experience and is developed primarily through peer-to-peer student communication.

What Is the Intent of Mathematical Practice 6?

As you study the expectations for Mathematical Practice 6, you will notice several areas for student proficiency, including:

1. Students communicate precisely to others.

2. Students use clear definitions of terms in discussing their reasoning.

3. Students express numerical answers with a degree of precision appropriate for the problem context.

4. Students calculate accurately and efficiently.

5. Students are careful about specifying units of measure and using proper labels.

Your role as a leader of instruction is to ensure precise student communication occurs during the lesson. Student problem solving includes the proper development and use of definitions; the appropriate use of symbols, most notably the equal sign; the specification of units along with the associated quantities; and the inclusion of clear and concise student explanations when describing solutions or task pathways.

An expectation of Mathematical Practice 6 is that you will observe students being accurate and appropriate with procedures and calculations. Accuracy is self-explanatory, but appropriateness as it relates to precision is a bit more elusive. Part of solving problems provided in context involves determining the level of precision that is necessary. Sometimes an estimate is sufficient, yet how close of an estimate is warranted or acceptable? The level of accuracy for measurements is often determined by the context of the problem and should be part of the collaborative discussion during the unit. Is the teacher crystal clear about the expectations he or she has for student precision?

How Can the Collaborative Team Address Mathematical Practice 6?

Teachers play a vital role in helping students attend to precision since students often emulate their teachers when they are not precise with definitions, general language, and expectations for solution presentations. Teachers need to be careful of the messages they send students at all times through mathematics instruction. Reaching agreement on language usage at the collaborative team level is an appropriate use of the teachers' professional learning community collaborative team time. Figure 2.4 (page 34) highlights questions that teachers should discuss within their collaborative teams when planning lessons to assess the precision quality of problem solving within a common or shared mathematical task.

---

1. What is the essential student vocabulary for this unit, and how will our team assess it?

2. What are the expectations for precision in student solution pathways, explanations, and labels during this unit?

3. How will students be expected to accurately describe the procedures they use to solve tasks and problems in class?

4. Will student work as it relates to in- and out-of-class problems and tasks require students to perform calculations carefully and appropriately?

5. Will students' team and whole-class discussions reveal an accurate use of mathematics?

Figure 2.4: Team planning questions that promote CCSS Mathematical Practice 6.

Visit **go.solution-tree.com/commoncore** for a reproducible version of this figure.

For example, consider the following rather simple mathematical task.

> Determine the distance between home plate and second base on a Major League Baseball field. Show all of your work, and provide an explanation.

Each teacher on a collaborative team could have a different response to both the problem solving and precision expectations for student solutions to this problem. When teachers share ideas (collaborate) in how to develop student precision in problem solving, collaborative teams find their most meaningful work. In this case, the collaborative team needs to consider factors such as the following.

- Clear expectations to the students regarding proper use of mathematical knowledge, such as the Pythagorean theorem or 45-45-90 right triangles

- Explanation rubrics on a scale of 1–4 (what type of student response would be a 4, 3, and so on?)

- Specificity of precision in the answer, such as an exact answer or an estimate, and if an estimate is acceptable, what type of estimate? Is $90\sqrt{2}$ feet OK? 127 feet? 127.27 feet? 127.2792 feet? 127 feet 3.35 inches? 127 feet 3⅓ inches?

- Consideration of extensions such as, How is the distance between home plate and second base actually measured? From the middle of each base or the back of home plate and the middle of second base, and how does that affect the answer? What is the actual measure provided in the Major League Baseball rulebook?

Your leadership role is to observe classrooms for opportunities for students (through meaningful problems and tasks such as the home plate to second base task) to explain and justify their mathematical ideas and engage in Mathematical Practice 6. You should also help teachers learn how to monitor students' work and discussions in order to provide corrective feedback to students and ensure precision development for all students in the grade level or the course.

Reasoning and Explaining

You observe reasoning in mathematics when you observe the means by which students try to make sense (by thinking through ideas carefully, considering examples and alternatives, asking questions, hypothesizing, pondering, and so on) of mathematics so it is usable and useful (NCTM, 2000). According to Ball and Bass (2003), "Mathematical reasoning is something that students can learn to do" (p. 33). In fact, these authors suggest two very important benefits of reasoning: (1) reasoning aids students' mathematical understanding and ability to use concepts and procedures in meaningful ways, and (2) reasoning helps students reconstruct *faded knowledge*—that is, knowledge that students forget but teachers can restore through reasoning with the current content.

Mathematical Practice 2: Reason Abstractly and Quantitatively

Mathematical Practice 2, "Reason abstractly and quantitatively," refers to the need for students to communicate precisely and correctly at every level of the mathematics curriculum —with teachers and, more specifically, with their peers (NGA & CCSSO, 2010, p. 6). This means that you must expect teachers to allow a significant amount of guided classroom time for peer-to-peer student interaction and discussion. The classroom lesson design should integrate small-step instruction as the teacher moves in and out of allowing for effective whole-group discussion and effective small-group student-team discussions.

What Is the Intent of Mathematical Practice 2?

Classroom discourse that promotes student reasoning involves teacher-to-student communication as well as student-to-student communication as essential elements of daily classroom lesson planning. Teacher-to-student communication might include questions from the teacher that probe students' thinking beyond student suggestions of an answer (Stein et al., 2007). Teachers consider students' answers, whether right or wrong, so students have opportunities to stretch their thinking beyond the answer. This is often referenced as *whole group* discourse.

In addition, student-to-student communication can and should involve discussions emerging from students' hypotheses about a mathematical concept or procedure and their propositions on how mathematics works. Student-to-student communication is supported by peer-to-peer explanations and debates as students are required to provide justification for their thinking. This is often referenced as *small group* discourse.

Mathematical Practice 2 contains several areas for student proficiency, including:

1. Students can decontextualize a problem by representing the problem symbolically for a solution.

2. Students can contextualize a problem by attending to the meaning of the quantities involved in the problem.

3. Students can create a coherent representation of the task or problem presented.

4. Students can attend to the meaning of the quantities involved in a problem as well the unit appropriate to the problem.

When students are engaged in Mathematical Practice 2, they are sharing and justifying their mathematical conceptions with the teacher and with *one another* as they adjust their thinking based on mathematical information gathered through discussions and responses to questions.

How Can the Collaborative Team Address Mathematical Practice 2?

To develop this type of student proficiency, your teacher teams should use common high-cognitive-demand tasks that are planned for as part of the unit. These tasks must be complemented by the use of well-prepared probing questions that assess students' current level of understanding, provide scaffolded support to students when they get stuck in the problem-solving process, and extend student reasoning for those students mastering the problem solutions as presented (Stein et al., 2007).

Figure 2.5 highlights questions that teachers should discuss within their collaborative teams when planning lessons to assess the quality of abstract reasoning within the common or shared mathematical tasks used during a unit of study.

---

1. What are the expectations for student reasoning and mathematical explanation for this problem or mathematical task?

2. How will students be expected to connect the problem's solutions and the limits on those solutions based on the context of the problem?

3. What are the questions teachers can ask if students get stuck in the problem? How can teachers scaffold the problem if necessary?

4. What are the nuances to the problem that can be extended (advancing questions) to student teams that demonstrate adequate solutions to the original task?

5. What are the prompts (scaffolding questions) teachers can use to help students teach, learn, and reason with one another during their work together on this problem or task?

Figure 2.5: Team planning questions that promote CCSS Mathematical Practice 2.

Visit **go.solution-tree.com/commoncore** for a reproducible version of this figure.

This Mathematical Practice is maximized and enhanced when you ensure that teachers allow students to work collaboratively to engage in the mathematical problems presented in class. Good tasks (that the teacher team generates) can fuel student-to-student discussion as students share their mathematical thinking and decision making about the routes their thinking should take in order to arrive at sensible solution. Students do this in teams under the watchful eye of the teacher as he or she tours the room and monitors progress and conversations. Through the careful analysis of student work and performance on various mathematics assessments, teachers can make inferences about students' ability to reason. Your role, once again, is to observe for the absence or presence of this student opportunity for practice and to help teachers grow in its daily use.

Mathematical Practice 3: Construct Viable Arguments and Critique the Reasoning of Others

The successful collaborative team facilitation of this standard is based on the social learning environment of the classroom. As Rasmussen, Yackel, and King (2003) note:

> Every class, from the most traditional to the most reform-oriented, has social norms that are operative for that particular class. What distinguishes one class from another is not the presence or absence of social norms but, rather, the nature of the norms that differ from class to class. (pp. 147–148)

What Is the Intent of Mathematical Practice 3?

Students engaged in Mathematical Practice 3, "Construct viable arguments and critique the reasoning of others," are making conjectures based on their analysis of given situations (NGA & CCSSO, 2010, pp. 6–7). Students explain and justify their thinking as they communicate to other classmates and the teacher. Classmates listen to explanations and justifications and judge the reasonableness of the claims. You should monitor classrooms weekly or monthly to ensure students are demonstrating this Mathematical Practice.

As you study the expectations for this Mathematical Practice, you will notice several areas for student proficiency including:

1. Students make conjectures and can explore the truth of those conjectures.

2. Students justify their conclusions and communicate them to others.

3. Students compare the effectiveness of two plausible arguments.

4. Students listen, read, and respond to the arguments of others for sense making and clarity.

When students are engaged in Mathematical Practice 3 they are making and evaluating their conjectures as part of meaningful discussions with their peers. This should be a daily occurrence in every mathematics lesson.

How Can the Collaborative Team Address Mathematical Practice 3?

Use figure 2.6 (page 38) to highlight questions teachers should discuss within their collaborative teams. These questions will help your teams plan lessons that assess how students will be expected to construct arguments and critique others' reasoning during class. Eventually, these types of student conjectures and peer discussions should become a natural part of the classroom discourse *every day*. When well managed, they can occur in an organized way with limited teacher direction. These norms are established through a process of negotiation in which the teacher makes his or her expectations clear, but involves students in the process of implementing the norms (Cobb, 2000). These sorts of rules are necessary to support what effective mathematics learners *do* in the classroom each day. Mathematics learners make conjectures, test those conjectures, and discuss their implications within a community that is receptive to such discussions. Your role as a leader is to support your collaborative teams to design structures (norms) that allow for this type of student community. For example, you can help teachers design a set of

1. How will students provide explanations and justifications as part of their solution processes during class activities?

2. How will students attempt to make sense of their classmates' solutions by asking questions for clarification of their peers?

3. How will students communicate disagreements when they don't understand or don't agree with solutions presented by others, spurring discussion between and among students?

4. How will the lesson design allow and encourage students to make conjectures about new information and test the validity of those conjectures?

Figure 2.6: Team planning questions that promote CCSS Mathematical Practice 3.

Visit **go.solution-tree.com/commoncore** for a reproducible version of this figure.

student *rights* ("You have a right to ask for help from a peer") and *responsibilities* ("You have a responsibility to help others"). As an example, note the following strategies for student engagement during small-group discourse (Chapin & O'Connor, 2007).

- Have a student paraphrase or summarize a student response or strategy, and ask others to verify the first student's summary.

- Direct a student question to the class, or ask another student to respond.

- Ask another student or student team if they agree or disagree with the statement of a student or team and why.

- Ask a student or student team to explain something in a different way.

The teacher's level of specialized content knowledge should be such that he or she is able to use high-cognitive-demand problems to elicit conjectures and arguments and to guide discussions around important mathematical ideas. When there is disagreement regarding a solution, the student making the claim needs classroom time to explain his or her thinking to peers—usually best facilitated in small-group student discourse. The student critiquing the claim makes sense of the argument and then provides clarification including another justification. You should communicate to teachers that you expect small-group student discourse around a high-cognitive-demand task almost every day. At a minimum, collaborative teams should outline a plan for how to make this become a practiced reality throughout each unit.

Modeling and Using Tools

One major teacher role in mathematics is to establish *relevance* with students. Relevance in mathematics requires the teacher and the collaborative team to provide opportunities for students to explore and share solutions to real-world situations that present themselves in and out of daily school life. The classroom tasks used should be conducive to the sorts of discourse described in Mathematical Practice 3—Construct viable arguments and critique the reasoning of others. These two Mathematical Practices for modeling and using tools also serve and connect to Mathematical Practice 1—Make sense of problems and persevere in solving them, and Mathematical Practice 2—Reason abstractly and quantitatively, with its focus on "mathematizing" real-world problems.

In many ways, your collaborative teams may need your help in understanding that the Standards for Mathematical Practice are intricately connected. Planning for student growth and proficiency in Mathematical Practices 4 and 5 is dependent on teachers planning for and implementing the other practices as well. Additionally, students can't become better at modeling with mathematics or using tools strategically if they are not allowed to engage in and practice tasks that require such actions. Your role then is to ensure collaborative team unit and lesson-plan design that accommodates these student practices.

Mathematical Practice 4: Model With Mathematics

Students engaged in CCSS Mathematical Practice 4, "Model with mathematics," solve real-world problems by applying known mathematics arising from everyday life, society, and the workplace (NGA & CCSSO, 2010, p. 7).

What Is the Intent of Mathematical Practice 4?

In this practice, students represent mathematical concepts by using various tools to model and make sense of the mathematics. More generally, students use symbols and tools to represent real-world situations and move fluidly between different representations based on the questions they are trying to answer. The ways students model and represent situations using tools will evolve as students learn more sophisticated mathematics. A goal is for students to model mathematics in order to become more mathematically proficient.

As you study the expectations for Mathematical Practice 4, you will notice several areas for student proficiency including:

1. Students represent mathematical concepts by using such tools as diagrams, tables, charts, graphs, calculators, graphing calculators, and various forms of area or volume models.

2. Students use symbols and tools to represent real-world situations.

3. Students routinely interpret their mathematical results in the context of the problem situation.

4. Students are comfortable making assumptions and approximations to simplify a complicated real-life situation and are comfortable testing those assumptions.

Students must first be given the opportunity to explore real-world problems or situations and then be encouraged to represent those problems mathematically. Once students represent the problems with mathematics they should solve the problems and interpret their results within the context of the problem. All of this depends on the students being provided the opportunity to solve problems that arise from everyday life. These sorts of experiences will prepare students for expectations related to reasoning mathematically (NCTM, 2009). Monitor team agendas for the presence of this important unit-by-unit outcome, and respond as needed. Collaborative teams should include this in their lesson design and planning work.

How Can the Collaborative Team Address Mathematical Practice 4?

By providing opportunities for students to develop real-world contexts to correspond to mathematics tasks of varying difficulty, and then to check to make sure the correspondence is accurate, teachers facilitate students' sense making relative to modeling mathematics. Students need to be active participants in using mathematics to make sense of daily life. They can use symbols and tools to help them make sense of and solve naturally arising problems in reasonable ways. Figure 2.7 provides one way you can help your collaborative teams plan lessons that honor this Standard for Mathematical Practice.

Thinking about the world in mathematical ways may take effort for some. Spend a week or two making this a priority with the goal of making it a habit. Appropriate mathematical problems to explore can present themselves in unexpected situations.

1. Keep a list of the real-world mathematics problems you identify online, in newspapers, and so on.

2. Share and explore the problems with your collaborative team for connections to the unit content.

3. Work in your collaborative team to come up with (and solve) additional problems related to the scenarios that the team shares.

4. Determine the tools necessary to help students explore the real-world mathematical problem or task your team designs.

Figure 2.7: Collaborative team task for modeling and using tools.

Visit **go.solution-tree.com/commoncore** for a reproducible version of this figure.

In order for teachers to be comfortable with this standard, they need to explore such representations themselves and within their collaborative team to understand the nuances of the problem, the setup, the solution, and the computation or symbolic manipulation involved. Students engaged in this Mathematical Practice will not only check for reasonableness of the computation but will also extend sense making to determine if the solution is appropriate given the original problem context.

Consider the sample mathematics problem in figure 2.8. Students are asked to make a conjecture about a Wikipedia claim that could be used as a common team task during a unit that addresses certain standards from the Number and Quantity conceptual category. Students are expected to work together in teams and use their mathematical knowledge and understanding to justify their solution. In the process, students must be clear about the units they are using for representing various quantities, such as people, restaurants, or meals. The role of the teacher is to facilitate the conversations in the classroom so students are respectfully critiquing each other's claims and justifications. If you observe that students are unaccustomed to challenging others' thinking, you should be prepared to help the teacher develop questions to ask students in teams, such as, "Can you replicate the work of your peer? If not, what additional questions do you have for the student?"

Wikipedia reports that 8 percent of all Americans eat at McDonald's every day. Data reveal approximately 311 million Americans in 2012 and 12,800 McDonald's restaurants in the United States.

Make a conjecture as to whether or not you believe the web release to be true, and then create a mathematical argument that justifies your conclusion.

Figure 2.8: Sample conjecture about a Wikipedia claim.

Visit **go.solution-tree.com/commoncore** for a reproducible version of this figure.

The McDonald's Wikipedia problem presented in figure 2.8 is an example that can be expanded or altered to lend itself to modeling of mathematics. Students might be given data about the consumption of meals at McDonald's for several years and asked to predict the American consumption of meals at McDonald's in 2020. In such a problem, your collaborative teams anticipate student strategies and questions and determine how much scaffolding to provide students. Teachers could also give students the problem task in figure 2.8 and ask them to explore related questions that might require the development of a mathematical model to predict future trends. As an instructional leader, you could take part in the team discussion about the McDonald's problem and other problems like it. If you do, you will also discover the required connection to Mathematical Practice 5.

Mathematical Practice 5: Use Appropriate Tools Strategically

The nature of mathematics facilitates the use of a variety of tools for teaching and learning. Every mathematics classroom should be equipped to accommodate Mathematical Practice 5, "Use appropriate tools strategically" (NGA & CCSSO, 2010, p. 7).

What Is the Intent of Mathematical Practice 5?

Hands-on, active, and concrete learning supports this Mathematical Practice. For students, this standard is not about watching the teacher demonstrate various tools. Specifically, this practice is about students *experiencing* the use of tools. This gives students an opportunity to develop understanding by engaging in applications involving mathematics. In fact, some CCSS content cannot be sufficiently explored unless students have access to proper tools.

In order for students to select appropriate tools, those tools first have to be made available to them. The McDonald's problem in figure 2.8 (like most real-life models) is difficult to do without some type of calculation tool. Your collaborative teams should have an effective plan for acquiring or providing access to tools and an effective system for students to use those tools. In order for this Mathematical Practice to be implemented, you might need to provide support and funding so that every teacher can acquire and use necessary tools to benefit all students of a grade level or course. In a nutshell, a variety of technology and nontechnology tools should be readily available to students to support mathematical explorations that highlight the development of student understanding.

As you study the expectations for Mathematical Practice 5, you will notice several areas for student proficiency including:

1. Students choose an appropriate tool for the problems and tasks presented in class and homework. Is the tool necessary to the mathematical task or problem?

2. Students know the limits of each tool for providing accurate solutions to the problem.

3. Students detect tool-generated errors by estimating reasonable solutions without the tool.

4. Students use tools to explore and deepen their discovery and understanding of concepts.

Once teachers make sure a variety of tools are available to students, it is important to provide students with support in selecting appropriate tools for a particular mathematics task. In addition, by providing guidance instead of selecting tools for students, teachers will provide space for students to make hypotheses, try new ways of studying mathematics, and have a context for comparing how different tools can either be useful or a hindrance for studying the specific mathematics involved in the task—such as the McDonald's task and the acceptable presentation of student work for the task.

How Can the Collaborative Team Address Mathematical Practice 5?

Teachers can find it very enjoyable to teach mathematics with a variety of tools. However, the real issue for the collaborative team is whether the tools support student learning —tools should not be used for the sake of using tools (technology tools included). If students use tools to engage in mathematics and walk away from the experience with little or no understanding of the mathematics, then the use of the tools was ineffective and potentially a waste of valuable resources and time.

Figure 2.9 highlights questions for teacher teams to discuss when planning unit lessons that use tools strategically.

As we plan for the strategic use of tools during this unit, how will we ensure the following?

1. Student accuracy and coherence in displaying solution pathways

2. Student use of technology for dynamic or multiple mathematical representations of the concept

3. Student collection and dissemination of formative assessment data generated by the tool

4. Student use of collaborative learning and sharing with peers to discuss their reasoning and thinking using the tools

5. Questions that probe students' thinking before, during, and after students use tools to study the mathematics in the lesson and determine when a particular tool may be useful

---

Figure 2.9: Team planning considerations that promote CCSS Mathematical Practice 5.

Visit **go.solution-tree.com/commoncore** for a reproducible version of this figure.

As you observe mathematics teaching and observe and support collaborative team planning discussions, do you "see" any of these five considerations in place? One of your roles as an instructional leader requires you to know what you are seeing as well as what you are *not* seeing and to close the gap between the two. Discussing the effective use of technology and other types of tools for students to use as they reason mathematically must become an integral part of your leadership expectations for the collaborative work and decisions of your collaborative teams on a unit-by-unit basis throughout the year.

Teachers are supporting Mathematical Practice 5 when you observe them asking students if their answers are reasonable, facilitating the classroom discourse that allows students to learn from each other, and ensuring that students make sense of their answers according to the context of the problem. Thus, Mathematical Practice 5 can and should be used as a lever to support student development in the first four Mathematical Practices.

Seeing Structure and Generalizing

A major contribution to the inherent beauty in mathematics is its structure. Structure exists all across the mathematics curriculum. Consider structure in geometry (every square is a rhombus), basic operations (an even number plus an even number always results in a sum that is an even number), and numerical patterns (1, 4, 9, 16, and so on). Structure can help students learn what to expect in mathematics. If students learn how mathematics works and why it works the way it does, they then begin to notice, look for, and make use of structure to solve more difficult tasks and problems as they become engaged in what it means to *do* mathematics. Seeing structure and generalizing are usually difficult Mathematical Practices to develop in students. It will take significant professional development with your mathematics leaders to move these practices into the mainstream of teacher planning.

Mathematical Practice 7: Look For and Make Use of Structure

Students engaged in CCSS Mathematical Practice 7, "Look for and make use of structure," are presented tasks conducive to exploring structure and provided opportunities to create examples of structure to share and discuss with each other (NGA & CCSSO, 2010, p. 8).

What Is the Intent of Mathematical Practice 7?

As you study the expectations for Mathematical Practice 7, you will notice several areas for student proficiency:

1. Students' attention is consistently drawn to the structure of the mathematics as it occurs. For example, the teacher consistently asks, "What do you notice is happening here? How does this compare to some of our previous experiences?"

2. Students are engaged in exploring numerical and visual patterns that reveal the structure. For example, the teacher engages students in an exploration across

representations that require students to conjecture about the connections and structure within the problem.

3. Students can use strategies that shift the perspective of a problem—like an auxiliary line in geometry. As an example, when exploring mathematical structure involving zero or negative exponents, why does $2^{-3} = \frac{1}{8}$? Students can explore the pattern, $2^4 = 16$, $2^3 = 8$, $2^2 = 4$, and $2^1 = 2$. In order to preserve the structure of the pattern, students can discern that 2^0 must equal 1, 2^{-1} must equal ½, and so on as the pattern continues in order to preserve the structure of the properties of exponents.

How Can the Collaborative Team Address Mathematical Practice 7?

Figure 2.10 highlights questions teachers should discuss within their collaborative teams when planning how to assess student development of structure during certain lessons in the unit.

As we plan for the student discernment of structure during this unit:

1. What is the mathematical structure present in this unit?

2. Which lessons during this unit offer an opportunity to reveal the structure of the mathematics to the students?

3. Can we create lesson prompts that reveal the structure that exists in this unit?

4. Can we create lesson prompts that allow students to discern the structure that exists in this unit?

5. Can we use an a-ha moment or student investigation moment around a numerical, visual, or algebraic pattern that reveals the structure?

6. Can students use collaborative learning and sharing with peers using tools that allow for a dynamic understanding of the structure from a variety of settings and perspectives in a way that is efficient?

Figure 2.10: Team planning questions that promote CCSS Mathematical Practice 7.

Visit **go.solution-tree.com/commoncore** for a reproducible version of this figure.

Using tools strategically as described in Mathematical Practices 4 and 5 is often a great way to either visualize the structure or allow for a dynamic student investigation into the structure that exists in the mathematical task. Your role as a school leader is not so much to need to know the mathematics and its attending structure as much as it is to ensure that your collaborative team designs and implements lessons that ask students to observe or inspect the structure involved in learning the content standards for the unit's lessons. You can do this by observing the types of questions or student activities outlined in figure 2.10. As students become more confident recognizing structure, and as teachers model for students the mathematical connections and relevance that comes from using structure in mathematics, classroom instruction has the potential to become more meaningful for students.

Mathematical Practice 8: Look For and Express Regularity in Repeated Reasoning

When engaged in CCSS Mathematical Practice 8, "Look for and express regularity in repeated reasoning," you should observe students moving beyond just solving problems to get answers to finding ways to generalize the methods they use and to determining *efficient methods* for those procedures (NGA & CCSSO, 2010, p. 8).

What Is the Intent of Mathematical Practice 8?

As you study the expectations for Mathematical Practice 8, you will notice two primary areas for student proficiency:

1. Students notice and discuss if their results seem reasonable while solving the problem and when they've solved the problem.

2. Students notice and can articulate patterns in calculations that can become generalized properties or formulas.

As an example, with a desire to simplify students' learning pathways and minimize confusion (Stigler et al., 1999), teachers are often tempted to provide students with efficient procedures for number or algebraic computations too early. When this occurs, students miss the opportunity to look for and express regularity in repeated reasoning.

How Can the Collaborative Team Address Mathematical Practice 8?

You can use figure 2.11 to highlight questions teachers should discuss within their collaborative teams when planning lessons to assess how students will be expected to look for and express regularity in repeated reasoning.

We need to plan for student investigations and provide students with opportunities to make sense of problems and look for the regularity in the calculations.

1. How can we develop this student practice simultaneously with Mathematical Practices 1 and 7?

2. How can we create and design tasks that allow for students to develop perseverance to make sense of repeated reasoning?

3. How can we avoid teaching shortcuts or memorized procedures (various mnemonics) before students build complete understanding of the mathematical skill or procedure involved?

4. What types of examples and counterexamples can we provide to help students to notice if patterns repeat?

Figure 2.11: Team planning questions that promote CCSS Mathematical Practice 8.

Visit **go.solution-tree.com/commoncore** for a reproducible version of this figure.

Asking students to describe the processes they use and to look for repetition in those processes provides the scaffolding necessary for students to make sense of the process of determining general methods for calculations. It is important that these patterns and the structures that adjoin them are explored in order to develop understanding of the reasonableness of calculated solutions. For example, ask, "Why is 2^{-3} a positive number?" As you observe mathematics lessons and ensure for student understanding, you should look for teacher questions like, "Why is this true? What do you notice? How is this pattern similar to others we have examined in the past? How does extending the problem to include _____ change our perspective?"

Once again, the classroom environment and expectations the teacher establishes related to social interactions in the classroom set the stage for students to engage in this practice. The dynamic nature of exploring problems or tasks using various tools will also facilitate efficient classroom time and engagement in this Mathematical Practice. If there is an expectation that students will make conjectures about the structure related to what they notice in the calculations and patterns they complete, students are more likely to look for and make sense of those generalizations. Your role as a leader is to ensure there is an expectation that students will create generalizations and then defend them as well as consider potential counterexamples. Thus, students will have the opportunity to create general methods for repeated reasoning. This is an expectation for all students K–12.

Lesson-Design Elements That Reflect the Common Core Mathematical Practices

Typically in preservice training, teachers are taught lesson-design elements. This lesson design is usually quite extensive and several pages long, serving the intended purpose of allowing the professor or cooperating teacher the opportunity to provide meaningful feedback. However, in actual practice, limited time and experience make this practice cumbersome. Nonetheless, the preservice lesson plans often contain important and useful elements including connection to state standards, the lesson tasks and learning targets, student prerequisite knowledge, lesson details (warm-up or bell ringer, end-of-lesson summary, and so on), and an assessment strategy.

At some point, usually early in their careers, teachers make their lesson plans much more abbreviated. Whereas teachers typically give consideration to key components of the lesson, these considerations are often not recorded or tracked. Yet without a way to document critical elements of the lesson design and the teacher thinking that went into its creation, collaborative dialogue with your colleagues around meaningful instruction is challenging, if not impossible.

In many schools, the details and specifics of the overall lesson design often varies widely from teacher to teacher in the same mathematics department or grade level. Is that the case in your school or district? Nevertheless, certain design elements are known to be essential in the creation of mathematics lessons that ensure each student is engaged in the expectations of learning the CCSS for mathematics throughout the class period.

Teachers' lesson-design elements should also be based on instructional strategies that research has shown to have a positive impact on student achievement. In his book *Qualities of Effective Teachers*, Stronge (2007) notes, "Effective teachers recognize that no single instructional strategy can be used in all situations" (p. 69). Rather, highly effective collaborative teacher teams develop a toolbox of various methods to be used to differentiate instruction. Although there is no single best prescriptive way to teach mathematics, we present three lesson-design tools that provide guidelines for teacher planning and lesson design that include both teacher and student reflecting behaviors (indicators).

To pursue the eight CCSS Mathematical Practices as a reality in your school or district, you should expect each of your collaborative teams to be able to provide you with evidence of lesson-planning design elements that highlight consistent focus on and energy of the Mathematical Practices. Table 2.1 presents lesson-design elements your teams should use at the beginning, during, and at the end of a unit to achieve stage seven collaboration (see table 1.1, page 12). Combining essential elements of effective instruction and drawing from the collective expectations of the CCSS Mathematical Practices, table 2.1 provides teachers general guidelines and questions to use as they work to create and reflect on unit lesson designs that represent the spirit and intent of the CCSS for mathematics (Marzano, 2007; Marzano, Pickering, & Heflebower, 2010; Smith & Carter, 2007, as cited in Smith & Stein, 2011; Stiggins, 2007; Stronge, 2007).

Table 2.1: Elements of an Effective Mathematics Classroom Lesson Design

	Probing Questions for Effective Lesson Design	Reflection
1. Lesson Context: Learning Targets **Procedural Fluency** *and* **Conceptual Understanding Balancing**	What is the learning target for the lesson? How does it connect to the bigger focus of the unit?	
	What evidence will be used to determine the level of student learning of the target?	
	Are conceptual understanding and procedural fluency appropriately balanced?	
	How will you formatively assess student conceptual understanding of the mathematics concepts *and* of the procedural skill?	
	What meaningful application or model can you use?	
	Which CCSS Mathematical Practices will be emphasized during this lesson?	

continued →

	Probing Questions for Effective Lesson Design	Reflection
2. Lesson Process: High-Cognitive-Demand Tasks **Planning Student Discourse and Engagement**	What tasks will be used that create an a-ha student moment and leave "mathematical residue" (insights into the mathematical structure of concepts) regardless of content type at a high-cognitive-demand level?	
	How will you ensure the task is accessible to all students while still maintaining a high cognitive demand for students?	
	What strategic mathematical tools will be used during the lesson?	
	How will each lesson *example* be presented and sequenced to build mathematical reasoning connected to prior student knowledge?	
	What are the assessing and advancing questions you might ask during guided, independent, or group practice? What are anticipated student responses to the examples or tasks?	
	How might technology and student attention to precision play a role in the student lesson experience?	
3. Introduction, Daily Review, and Closure	What activity will be used to immediately engage students at the beginning of the class period?	
	How can the daily review be used to provide brief, meaningful feedback on homework? (Five minutes maximum)	
	How will the students summarize the lesson learning targets and the key vocabulary words?	

	Probing Questions for Effective Lesson Design	Reflection
4. Homework	How does the homework assignment provide variety and meaning to the students—including long-term review and questions—that balance procedural fluency with conceptual understanding?	

Visit **go.solution-tree.com/commoncore** for a reproducible version of this table.

Table 2.1 highlights essential lesson-design components for teacher team planning and discussion. You can use these components to guide teacher planning of effective mathematics lessons as well as for collaborative team reflection and modifications after a lesson, or a group of lessons, in a unit. Teachers should use the guiding questions from table 2.1 to lead the collaborative team in a more sophisticated dialogue centered on critical issues in lessons that get at the heart of teaching a standard well and accounting for the elements critical to the overall classroom design before, during, and after the lesson. The process of teacher discussion and reflection on lesson design—success and failure—is also part of the five-step teaching-assessing-learning cycle that will be discussed in chapter 4.

With your leadership, as teachers and teacher teams collaborate during a unit of instruction to design effective mathematics lessons, they should consider the design elements outlined in table 2.1: lesson context; lesson process; introduction, daily review, and closure; and homework.

Design Element One: Lesson Context

The lesson-design process begins with identifying the lesson context. Key elements must be established prior to delving into the intricacies of the actual classroom activities. Teachers must be explicit about mathematical concepts and processes that will guide the lesson. The context of the lesson is the driving force for the entire lesson-design process. The lesson context is about being clear on the content and processes students are to learn.

The crux of the lesson rests on the collaborative team identifying the CCSS *learning target* of the lesson to be taught. The learning target articulates for students what they are to learn and at the same time provides insight as to how students will be assessed. Although learning targets might be developed as part of curriculum writing or review, stage seven (see table 1.1, page 12) takes time during lesson design to make sure the learning target clearly communicates to students the key content and level of reasoning on which they will be assessed (Stiggins, Arter, Chappuis, & Chappuis, 2006).

Traditionally, typical mathematics instruction focused on procedures and cursory knowledge of mathematical content only (Hiebert et al., 2003). For several years, a war of sorts raged as to whether teaching mathematics should emphasize procedural fluency or conceptual understanding. This is not an *either/or* proposition. It is an *and* requirement. Both have a place in the teaching and learning of meaningful mathematics (Brown, Seidelmann, & Zimmermann, 2006; National Mathematics Assessment Panel [NMAP], 2008). The CCSS for mathematics (NGA & CCSSO, 2010) and NCTM (2000, 2008a) agree that procedural fluency is important but must be developed with understanding, reasoning, and critical thinking. In general, student procedural fluency development should rest on a *foundation of conceptual understanding* of learning targets.

Design Element Two: Lesson Process

According to Siegler (2003), analytical thinking leads to purposeful engagement and vice versa. In other words, when students are asked to make sense, they engage, and when students engage, they are trying to make sense. Students' interaction with the content and processes is vital to learning, and through the interaction between the teacher, students, and the content, meaning is made of mathematical knowledge and ways of reasoning (Cobb, Yackel, & Wood, 1992). Fundamental to mathematics instruction is carefully choosing tasks that support and encourage student reasoning about the content. Thus, your collaborative teams are obligated to design "worthwhile mathematical tasks" that engage students to "make connections and develop a coherent framework for mathematical ideas" (Martin, 2007, p. 32). Tasks need to highlight problem solving and mathematical reasoning in ways that "do not separate mathematical thinking from mathematical concepts and skills" (Martin, 2007, p. 33). Your role is to ensure every member of a collaborative team designs and uses *common* high-cognitive-demand tasks in every unit. When teachers fail to do so, they create inequity in student learning within the same grade level or course.

Selecting Common and High-Demand Tasks

Stein, Smith, Henningsen, and Silver (2009) define the cognitive demand of a task as "the kind and level of thinking required of students in order to successfully engage with and solve a task" (p. 1). They further identify low-level-cognitive-demand tasks as memorizing or applying procedures without connections. High-level-cognitive-demand tasks are procedures with connections or what the authors call *doing mathematics*, whereby students engage in more complex reasoning, analyzing, and problem solving. The learning target of the lesson dictates the cognitive level of task. If the learning target is for students to develop fluency, low-level-cognitive-demand tasks are appropriate. However, if students only work through tasks of low-level cognitive demand, they do not develop the connected and deep mathematical understanding needed to apply their knowledge in new situations.

As you observe mathematics lessons be sure to observe the level of task demand. As Stein et al. (2009) note, "Students also need opportunities on a regular basis to engage with tasks that lead to deeper, more generative understandings regarding the nature of mathematical processes, concepts, and relationships" (p. 5). The cognitive demand of tasks matters and is related to gains in student achievement at the classroom level even after controlling for socioeconomic status (Schmidt, Cogan, Houang, & McKnight, 2011).

Once teacher teams have determined the instructional goal and selected appropriate student tasks, you may need to help teachers learn how to anticipate likely student responses—and provide support for preparing at-the-ready *assessing* and *advancing* questions that will help students either get unstuck or drill deeper into the problem.

When teachers are prepared for and anticipate students' responses, they can monitor student work, watch and listen, and coach student responses efficiently. Through your observations, you can see whether teachers increase or decrease the cognitive demand associated with a task and provide feedback. When teachers succumb to students' demands to break down tasks and make them more explicit, they deny students the opportunity to engage in the sense-making aspects of the task and rob students of the opportunity to develop deep mathematical understandings (Stein et al., 2007).

Teachers should be encouraged to engage their students with *productive struggle*— students should come to expect that expending effort to learn mathematics is worthwhile and necessary (Hiebert & Grouws, 2007). Productive struggle characterizes Mathematical Practice 1. It is your leadership role, partially, to help the teacher think and plan for moves that produce this type of "productive struggle" in class.

Planning and Implementing Student Discourse and Engagement

If the only experience students have in the mathematics classroom is working independently without collaborating with their peers, students will not be able to meet the vision of any of the eight CCSS Mathematical Practices. It is your leadership responsibility to ensure this is not the case. Through the discourse and the articulation of one's thinking, students create meaning and make connections. Students who listen to each other's strategies and critique each other's reasoning learn more. When students are working together to learn, the collaborative effort "enhances problem solving and reasoning to a greater degree than working independently would achieve" (Wood, Bruner, & Ross, 1976, as cited in Siegler, 2003, p. 298).

Forman (2003) asserts that when students work together to reason, problem solve, and communicate about mathematics, it has a "profound influence on children's learning processes and outcomes . . . includ[ing] motivational, affective, normative factors and involves beliefs about learning and goals for learning" (p. 347). Although there is a place for independent practice and learning, it is when students work together in a learning environment around carefully chosen tasks centered on meaningful mathematics that they develop shared and complex understandings of ideas, concepts, vocabulary, and symbols contained within the CCSS for mathematics. You must communicate this vision to all teachers so they understand this type of instruction, implement the vision, and learn how to orchestrate small-group student discourse in a way that is effective and expected for all students.

Design Element Three: Introduction, Daily Review, and Closure

You should observe to determine if teachers are designing beginning-of-class activities for immediate student engagement. Each collaborative team should discuss the goal and purpose for each daily opening activity. The activity could be used as a hook to grab the attention and curiosity of students about the upcoming lesson. The chosen activity might assess prerequisite knowledge for the day's lesson or assess what students know about a previous learning target. The initial activity might be used as a quick practice of standardized testing strategies or problems. Regardless of the goal of the opening activity, the idea is to immediately engage students in doing mathematics.

The opening activity can also be a time for teachers on the collaborative team to differentiate to best meet the needs of students in their respective classes. However, teachers should avoid doing homework review as an opening activity, since it is not the best way to engage students.

When you observe any type of review activity, ask yourself, "Who is doing all of the work during the going-over moments of class (going over homework, going over a test or quiz, going over a problem or task, or going over a practice problem)? Is it the teacher or the students?" If it is the teacher, help him or her restructure the activity. In your feedback communicate that review moments should occur in small-group discourse to promote a student-engaged activity. The opening activity should be brief to avoid a counterproductive cycle of wasted class time.

Whether the instructional period is thirty-two minutes or ninety minutes, some type of *student-led* closing to the lesson is crucial to summarize and highlight key concepts or ideas from the lesson. The closure can be as simple as asking students to share their thoughts about new ideas or how the day's lesson connects to lessons previously taught. Whether the closure is a whole-class question, a group reflection, or an individual task, an end-of-lesson summary refocuses students on important conceptual understandings and Mathematical Practices. Teachers and students each need to reflect on whether students met the learning target that was set for that day. As you observe, ask yourself, "Who is summarizing the lesson? The teacher, the student, or no one?" Make sure it is student work.

Design Element Four: Homework

There are several schools of thought about the role and extent of homework. Marzano (2007) finds that to have positive effect, homework should have a clear purpose that is communicated to students. The purpose of homework may be to deepen students' conceptual understanding, enhance procedural fluencies, or even to expose students to new content. Your teams should intentionally consider and choose each problem based on the learning target.

As a school leader, you should emphasize the importance of collaboratively planning mathematics homework. Homework for a unit of study must be a collaborative team–developed decision. Teams should determine the grade-level or course-based homework before the unit begins. Students should know of homework expectations in advance of the unit. Failure to design homework in a collaborative team results in inequity in teaching and learning. Through collaboratively planning and designing homework assignments, all students of a grade level or course receive the same assignments.

Completing homework is an opportunity for students to reflect on their learning while developing strategies to problem solve and persevere. (Chapter 4 presents a formative process for student learning through student self-reflection, goal setting, and action.) The mathematics is visible in the process of how the student worked through the problem. Answers do little to reveal the extent of student understanding or misconceptions.

There are many advantages for teachers to provide students the homework answers as part of a unit-by-unit common formative assessment experience. When students are only expected to provide an answer for homework (and not show all work), the message communicated is that the problems' solutions are valued over the *process* used to arrive at the solution. When teachers provide students with answers to the homework problems, students can check their solutions against the answers, and if their end result does not match the provided answer, they can rework the problem to find their error. In other words, students receive immediate and formative self-assessed feedback of their work. Moreover, a compelling reason to provide students the answers to the homework in advance of the assignment is the time saved reviewing the homework during the class period. Time is no longer needed to display answers as the expectation has been developed in students that it is their responsibility to check those answers and identify what they understand or what help they will need prior to entering class the next day.

The Mathematical Practices Lesson-Design Tools

A lesson-planning template like figure 2.12 can provide support for the vision of instruction in your school or district and can be a useful teacher team tool as teachers discuss daily lesson construction. Figure 2.12 provides an intentional focus on differentiating instructional planning, developing Mathematical Practices, and building the lesson around meaningful student tasks that are engaging and require communication. Figure 2.12 presents a sample template that breaks down the lesson design and ensures a focus on one or more of the eight Mathematical Practices.

Unit: Date: Lesson:	
Learning target: As a result of today's class, students will be able to _____	
Formative assessment: How will students be expected to demonstrate mastery of the learning target during in-class checks for understanding?	
Probing Questions for Differentiation on Mathematical Tasks	
Assessing Questions	**Advancing Questions**
(Create questions to scaffold instruction for students who are "stuck" during the lesson or the lesson tasks.)	(Create questions to further learning for students who are ready to advance beyond the learning target.)

Figure 2.12: CCSS Mathematical Practices lesson-planning tool.   continued →

Targeted Standard for Mathematical Practice: Which Mathematical Practice will be targeted for proficiency development during this lesson?		
Tasks (Tasks can vary from lesson to lesson.)	**What Will the Teacher Be Doing?** (How will the teacher present and then monitor student response to the task?)	**What Will the Students Be Doing?** (How will students be actively engaged in each part of the lesson?)
Beginning-of-Class Routines How does the warm-up activity connect to students' prior knowledge, or how is it based on analysis of homework?		
Task 1 How will the students be engaged in understanding the learning target?		
Task 2 How will the task develop student sense making and reasoning?		
Task 3 How will the task require student conjectures and communication?		
Closure How will student questions and reflections be elicited in the summary of the lesson? How will students' understanding of the learning target be determined?		

Visit **go.solution-tree.com/commoncore** for a reproducible version of this figure.

Regardless of the textbook or course materials used or the lesson content or unit standards to be addressed, this template provides a consistent planning for the how-to of the lesson—focused on the CCSS Mathematical Practices. The intention is for this planning tool to be used in conjunction with teachers' other lesson-planning tools from the district. For example, because this tool is focused on the Mathematical Practices, it does not include lesson components such as independent practice or homework.

Table 2.2 provides a final lesson-design tool you can use for teacher observation purposes. It is an example of a possible observer look-for tool with indicators of teacher and student behaviors that reflect evidence of the various Mathematical Practices. The table provides a brief summative expectation of what you or other peer observers would expect to see taking place in a classroom that is intentionally developing the Mathematical Practices as part of the lesson design. You might be able to embed some of these elements in your current instructional observation tools.

Table 2.2: Mathematical Practices—Look-Fors as Classroom Indicators

Mathematical Practice	Look-Fors: Classroom Indicators
Mathematical Practice 1: Make sense of problems, and persevere in solving them.	**Students:** Are engaged in solving problems and high-cognitive-demand tasks **Teacher:** Provides adequate time with formative feedback for students to discuss problem pathways and solutions with peers
Mathematical Practice 2: Reason abstractly and quantitatively.	**Students:** Are able to contextualize or decontextualize problems **Teacher:** Provides access to and uses appropriate representations (manipulative materials, drawings, or online renderings) of problems and asks questions focused on determining student reasoning
Mathematical Practice 3: Construct viable arguments, and critique the reasoning of others.	**Students:** Understand and use prior learning in constructing arguments **Teacher:** Provides opportunities for students to listen to or read the conclusions and arguments of others—as students discuss approaches and solutions to problems, the teacher encourages them to provide arguments for why particular strategies work and to listen and respond to the reasoning of others and asks questions to prompt discussions.
Mathematical Practice 4: Model with mathematics.	**Students:** Analyze and model relationships mathematically (such as when using an expression or equation) **Teacher:** Provides contexts for students to apply the mathematics learned
Mathematical Practice 5: Use appropriate tools strategically.	**Students:** Have access to and use instructional tools to deepen understanding (for example, manipulative materials, drawings, and technological tools) **Teacher:** Provides and demonstrates appropriate tools (like manipulatives)

continued →

Mathematical Practice	Look-Fors: Classroom Indicators
Mathematical Practice 6: Attend to precision.	**Students:** Recognize the need for precision in response to a problem and use appropriate mathematics vocabulary
	Teacher: Emphasizes the importance of precise communication, including appropriate use of mathematical vocabulary, and emphasizes the importance of accuracy and efficiency in solutions to problems, including use of estimation and mental mathematics, when appropriate
Mathematical Practice 7: Look for and make use of structure.	**Students:** Are encouraged to look for patterns and structure (for example, when using properties and composing and decomposing numbers) within mathematics
	Teacher: Provides time for students to discuss patterns and structures that emerge in a problem's solution
Mathematical Practice 8: Look for and express regularity in repeated reasoning.	**Students:** Reason about varied strategies and methods for solving problems and check for the reasonableness of their results
	Teacher: Encourages students to look for and discuss regularity in their reasoning

Source: Adapted from Kanold, Briars, & Fennell, 2012.
Visit **go.solution-tree.com/commoncore** for a reproducible version of this table.

The look-fors in table 2.2 are examples of the Mathematical Practices' intent and can be modified as you seek particular student and teacher behaviors across or within the content domains of the CCSS. These practices will not all be evident every day. Nonetheless, the practice the teacher or teacher team chooses for developmental focus during the lesson or unit should be evident.

You should consider using the Mathematical Practices as a frame to organize student and teacher expectations when completing informal leader or peer observations at your school site. As a result of team discussions and efforts to modify instruction, you may be interested in tracking team progress in implementing Common Core mathematics. As noted previously, the Common Core Look-Fors Mathematics app (http://splaysoft .com/CCL4s/Welcome.html) for the iPad or iPhone is an example of one tool that tracks the growth of a teacher's transition through the implementation of the Common Core State Standards. A tool for teachers and teacher leaders, this app provides for informal peer observation and is a source for data analysis related to teaching. The app's *crowd-sourcing* feature allows users to access the online resources that other educators have shared, evaluated, and tagged to the Common Core Content Standards for mathematics.

Looking Ahead

Although the Standards for Mathematical Practice are not content, per se, but rather ways for students to engage with the content, they cannot exist without the CCSS content standards. Planning therefore must simultaneously involve careful consideration of the mathematical content goals (learning targets) and of how the practices can be implemented during the lesson to aid students in developing deep understanding of the content standards. Chapter 3 will examine the unique characteristics and essential features of the Common Core mathematics content standards you will need to understand and support as teachers deepen their understanding. Chapter 4 will examine ways in which the CCSS content and the Mathematical Practices can and should become part of a formative assessment process.

Chapter 2 Extending My Understanding

1. How do you know if your school or district mathematics program has embraced teaching that emphasizes student understanding, communication, reasoning, and modeling? What evidence would you provide that this is true on a daily basis?

2. This chapter presents an instructional paradigm shift: teaching mathematics only for procedural fluency is insufficient. Student understanding of content and using student understanding as a precursor to developing procedural fluency in mathematics is the new vision. What percent of your current mathematics curriculum is taught for understanding versus procedural knowledge? How do you know?

3. The chapter uses two key questions to help collaborative teams develop an understanding of the eight CCSS Mathematical Practices.

   ○ What is the intent of this CCSS Mathematical Practice?

   ○ How can the collaborative team address this CCSS Mathematical Practice?

   As part of the collaborative teamwork throughout the year, ask your teams to first define the Mathematical Practice in their own words, construct meaning and examples for each Mathematical Practice, and generate ideas for how to support the Mathematical Practice in daily lesson and weekly unit design.

4. Ask your collaborative teams to choose an application problem from the textbook or course materials and answer the following.

   a. Does the problem meet the suggested criteria in figure 2.3 (page 32)? If not, how might your team change the problem?

   b. What approaches might students take, and what support might teachers provide without doing the problem for the students?

    c. Which Mathematical Practices might your team emphasize in the problem?

5. Creating classroom norms is a critical component of creating a classroom culture whereby students reason abstractly and quantitatively as they construct viable arguments and critique the reasoning of others (Mathematical Practices 2 and 3). How can you help your collaborative teams create and implement expectations for students about their role in explaining, justifying, and critiquing the mathematical reasoning of their peers?

6. Identifying common high-cognitive-demand tasks and working together to discuss anticipated student responses and possible instructional moves a teacher might use are critical teacher collaboration tasks. How can you help the teacher team understand the critical equity issue and importance of designing and using *common* tasks across the grade level or course?

7. The lesson-design components in table 2.1 (page 47) and figure 2.12 (page 53) are detailed and extensive. A collaborative team development of a lesson involving all components of the lesson design would involve rich, meaningful dialogue about mathematics teaching and learning. Your collaborative teams should begin lesson planning together as part of unit design by using a few of the components and then building more sophisticated lessons. How can you support teacher development and design of *effective lessons* together?

8. Communicating a growth mindset to students is a key motivational factor. Teacher words and actions have an impact on whether students perceive a classroom culture that emphasizes a growth or fixed mindset. As you observe teacher and student behaviors in the classroom, do you observe a classroom culture that believes all students can learn?

Online Resources

Visit **go.solution-tree.com/commoncore** for links to these resources.

- **Resource Roundups (PBS Teachers, n.d.; www.pbs.org/teachers/resource roundups):** This website includes a list of possible questions and teaching tips for developing mathematical thinking in the classroom.

- **Discourse: Questioning (National Council of Teachers of Mathematics, 2011; www.nctm.org/resources/content.aspx?id=6730&itemid=6730&linkident ifier=id&menu_id=598):** NCTM provides several resources to examine and support questioning strategies.

- **Mathematics Questioning Strategies (Standards Management System, n.d.; http://sms.sdcoe.net/SMS/ma/mathQuestionStrategy.asp):** The San Diego County Office of Education offers a resource on the art of questioning in mathematics.

- **Common Core Standards for Mathematical Practice (Inside Mathematics, 2011; http://insidemathematics.org/index.php/common-core-standards):** This site provides classroom videos and lesson samples designed to illustrate the Mathematical Practices in action.

- **Standards for Mathematical Practice (Common Core State Standards Initiative, 2011; www.corestandards.org/the-standards/mathematics /introduction/standards-for-mathematical-practice):** This site links the text of the eight Mathematical Practices to the selection on "Connecting the Standards for Mathematical Practice to the Standards for Mathematical Content."

- **NCTM Lessons (http://illuminations.nctm.org):** *Illuminations* provides standards-based resources that improve mathematics teaching and learning for all students. These materials illuminate the vision for school mathematics set forth in *Principles and Standards for School Mathematics, Curriculum Focal Points for Prekindergarten through Grade 8 Mathematics*, and *Focus in High School Mathematics: Reasoning and Sense Making*.

- **Tools for the Common Core Standards (http://commoncoretools .wordpress.com):** Follow Bill McCallum's blog about tools that are being developed to support the implementation of the CCSS.

- **Common Core Math Initiative (Maine West Mathematics Department, n.d.; https://sites.google.com/a/maine207.org/mw-math-department/home /common-core):** The Maine West Mathematics Department offers a collection of resources, articles, and blogs to support the CCSS for mathematics vision.

- **Handheld Graphing Technology in Secondary Mathematics (http:// education.ti.com/sites/UK/downloads/pdf/References/Done/Burrill,G .%2520(2002).pdf):** This resource synthesizes and provides peer-reviewed published research on the implications for classroom practice regarding the relationship between graphing calculator technology and improved student mathematics achievement.

- **Mathematics Common Core Coalition (www.nctm.org/standards/math commoncore):** The Mathematics Common Core Coalition provides expertise and advice on the effective implementation of the Common Core State Standards for mathematics. NCTM, NCSM, the Association of Mathematics Teacher Educators, the Association of State Supervisors of Mathematics, CCSSO, NGA, SBAC, and PARCC are members. The site offers member-endorsed Common Core materials and resources.

CHAPTER 3

Leading the Implementation of the Common Core Mathematics Content

The Standards for Mathematical Content are a balanced combination of procedure and understanding. Expectations that begin with the word "understand" are often especially good opportunities to connect the practices to the content.... In this respect, those content standards which set an expectation of understanding are potential "points of intersection" between the Standards for Mathematical Content and the Standards for Mathematical Practice.

—NGA & CCSSO

In this chapter, you will examine the content, language, organization, and expectations of the CCSS for your K–12 mathematics curriculum. This chapter helps you to better understand the content expectations described in the grade-level books for this series and helps you monitor your collaborative teams' ability to deliver on and implement the expectations of the CCSS for your mathematics program.

This chapter also describes your role in facilitating the implementation of a mathematics curriculum that meets the vision and the expectations of the CCSS content standards. Depending on your background (or comfort level) and interest in mathematics, it can be difficult to articulate your exact expectations for a high-quality mathematics program that mirrors and reflects the expectations of the CCSS for mathematics. However, your leadership can and should monitor the existence of a clearly articulated mathematics curriculum that is aligned with the standards.

The CCSS for mathematics provide the vision for what students should know and be able to do in elementary school, middle school, and high school. Your leadership pursuit is to ensure students engage in and demonstrate proficiency of the expected curriculum standards.

The *content* paradigm shift of the CCSS is *less is more,* with fewer standards to be taught in each grade level or course. Thus, *less* (fewer standards) provides an opportunity to meet the expectations of *more* (focused and deeper student learning with understanding) at every grade level and in every course. As you begin full implementation toward the CCSS learning targets, there should no longer be a "race to the finish in April" feeling for state assessment preparation. For example, grade 3 has thirty-three content standards (NGA & CCSSO, 2010). Many of these standards require students to demonstrate understanding, such as the first standard in the Number and Operations —Fractions domain (3.NF.1):

> Understand a fraction $1/b$ as the quantity formed by 1 part when a whole is partitioned into b equal parts; understand a fraction a/b as the quantity formed by a parts of size b. (NGA & CCSSO, 2010, p. 24)

Notice how the standard begins with the verb *understand*. This is typical of many of the K–12 mathematics content standards in the Common Core. Your school mathematics program will need to be committed to slowing down the curriculum in a way that allows all students to demonstrate this type of understanding as well as the procedural fluency the CCSS expect. Your role will be to ensure teachers participate in and act on collaborative discussions necessary for grade- or course-level content clarity and low teacher-to-teacher variance on the questions, Learn what? and Learn how? The curriculum design team in your school or district is the team of professionals responsible for aligning your current local mathematics curricula to the CCSS for mathematics standards —to be distinguished from previous curricula guides the school or district used.

The CCSS for mathematics provide you, as a school leader, with the catalyst and the opportunity to ensure every teacher fully implements research-based instruction and assessment around the right and focused mathematics content most essential for student learning at each grade level.

The CCSS K–12 Mathematics Curriculum Paradigm Shift

Since 1989, NCTM has been a leader in the development of curriculum standards. The council's landmark *Curriculum and Evaluation Standards for School Mathematics* (NCTM, 1989) influenced the development and realignment of state mathematics standards throughout the United States. NCTM's (2000) *Principles and Standards for School Mathematics* updated the *Curriculum and Evaluation Standards* and served as the blueprint for revised state standards throughout the 2000s; the K–8 *Curriculum Focal Points* (NCTM, 2006) and *Focus in High School Mathematics: Reasoning and Sense Making* (NCTM, 2009) focused the teaching and learning of mathematics content on student *understanding.* Visit **go.solution-tree.com/commoncore** for the online-only appendix "Changes in Mathematics Standards, 1989–2012," which lists additional details about the development of mathematics standards and the impact on the curriculum paradigm shift.

The standards set a rigorous definition of college and career readiness, not by expecting an excessive number of topics but by demanding that students develop a depth of understanding for the content that must be taught at each grade level. Remember that the primary content shift you must lead is *less is more.* There are fewer standards per year with more depth and more opportunities for student demonstration of understanding.

To develop your own understanding of the CCSS for mathematics, you can begin with an examination of the differences between the content expectations within the *Principles and Standards for School Mathematics* (PSSM; NCTM, 2000) and the Common Core

State Standards (NGA & CCSSO, 2010). One initial difference is the descriptive language used to define the standards. The CCSS content areas are referred to as *domains* rather than *content topics* or *strands*. Also, note that while the PSSM content topics are the same across all grades K–12, the content domains within the CCSS differ according to grade level; for instance, Counting and Cardinality appears only at the kindergarten level, and Number and Operations—Fractions has a three-year focus from grades 3–5. Table 3.1 illustrates these differences and shows content topics defined in the *Principles and Standards for School Mathematics* and the content domains and conceptual categories defined in the Common Core State Standards. It also provides an opportunity to determine professional development content needs and teacher comfort with the content domains and clusters.

Table 3.1: K–12 Mathematics Content—*Principles and Standards for School Mathematics* and the Common Core State Standards

PSSM—Content Topics Grades PreK–12	CCSS—Content Domains Grades K–5	CCSS—Content Domains Grades 6–8	CSSS—Conceptual Categories High School
Number and Operations	Counting and Cardinality (K only)	Ratios and Proportional Relationships (grades 6–7 only)	Number and Quantity
	Number and Operations in Base Ten	The Number System	
	Number and Operations—Fractions (grades 3–5 only)		
Algebra	Operations and Algebraic Thinking	Expressions and Equations	Algebra
Measurement		Functions (grade 8 only)	Functions
Geometry	Geometry	Geometry	Geometry
Data Analysis and Probability	Measurement and Data	Statistics and Probability	Statistics and Probability
			Modeling

As noted, NCTM (2006) led the *less is more* mathematics curriculum shift with its release of the *Curriculum Focal Points*. The *Curriculum Focal Points* were intended to serve as a discussion document for states, school districts, and local schools as they began a conversation around the more important or *focus* topics at particular grades for levels K–8. Many states saw the Focal Points as an opportunity for their school or school district to identify areas of curricular focus within particular grades and also to provide the grade-by-grade essentials for all students. In many ways, the Focal Points became a precursor to the Common Core State Standards. The CCSS highlight the *critical areas* of each grade level. Visit www.corestandards.org/the-standards/mathematics to access the CCSS for grades K–12.

Notice the fourth column of table 3.1 (page 63). Unlike the K–8 Common Core standards, which have defined standards for each grade level organized by domain, the mathematics standards for high school are organized into six *conceptual categories*. The conceptual categories provide a "coherent view of high school mathematics as a student's work with functions, for example, crosses a number of traditional course boundaries, potentially up through and including calculus" (NGA & CCSSO, 2010, p. 57). Similar to the K–8 standards, these high school conceptual categories are organized into domains and clusters.

Each grade-level book for this series provides teachers with a deep examination of the important content across each grade. As your collaborative teams begin the work of analyzing the content for their grades or courses, you can help them decide the amount of calendar time to allot for each domain area and for determining student learning experiences and progressions. There are four major areas of content analysis that will benefit the work of your collaborative teams:

1. Understanding the domains, content standard clusters, and learning progressions

2. Seeking adequate time to teach the content

3. Accessing appropriate technology and strategic tools

4. Implementing the CCSS content standards

Your leadership role is to ensure that members of your curriculum design teams and your grade-level or course-based collaborative teams address these four critical CCSS content issues. Your professional development efforts related to the CCSS mathematical content (domains and content standard clusters) should include teacher team responses to these four content analysis areas.

Understanding the CCSS Domains, Clusters, and Learning Progressions

As your teacher teams develop a shared understanding of the content to be taught at each grade level, they develop consistent curricular expectations, serve equity goals, and create ownership among all teachers (DuFour et al., 2010). The grade-level books for this series contain an activity designed to help collaborative teams analyze the content domains and clusters enabling them to develop a shared understanding of these elements of the CCSS for mathematics.

The activity is designed to help the CCSS content become more familiar. Using the full CCSS K–12 mathematics standards document as well as district-level curriculum maps and documents, teacher teams ask various understanding questions for the grade-level standards:

1. What content is familiar for each grade level or course? What is familiar in the content standard clusters for each domain?

2. What appears to be new content to this particular grade level or course based on prior standard expectations (*Principles and Standards for School Mathematics* [NCTM, 2000], state standards, and so on)? What's challenging for students and teachers? (This may include common misconceptions.)

3. What needs unpacking? What topics need emphasizing?

Tables 3.2 and 3.3 (pages 65–67) provide examples from grades 3–5 and high school. These templates provide an analysis tool your teacher teams can use to respond to the understanding questions. The analysis provides a beginning point for your discussions and work that should take place as your collaborative teams develop understanding of the CCSS grade-level and course-based expectations and the differences from current and past curriculum. The teacher teams need to be able to support consistent curricular priorities, common pacing, and the development of subsequent grade-level and course common assessment instruments that will align with the vision of the CCSS. Your leadership role is to foster open discussions of these topics and is critical to helping teachers understand the impact of the CCSS on their teaching and student learning.

Table 3.2: Sample Grade-by-Grade Analysis Tool—Grade 3

Content Standard Cluster	Which Standards in the Cluster Are Familiar?	What's New or Challenging in These Standards?	Which Standards in the Cluster Need Unpacking or Emphasizing?
Operations and Algebraic Thinking (3.OA)			
Represent and solve problems involving multiplication and division.			
Understand properties of multiplication and the relationship between multiplication and division.			
Multiply and divide within 100.			
Solve problems involving the four operations, and identify and explain patterns in arithmetic.			

continued →

Content Standard Cluster	Which Standards in the Cluster Are Familiar?	What's New or Challenging in These Standards?	Which Standards in the Cluster Need Unpacking or Emphasizing?
Number and Operations in Base Ten (3.NBT)			
Use place-value understanding and properties of operations to perform multidigit arithmetic.			
Number and Operations—Fractions (3.NF)			
Develop understanding of fractions as numbers.			
Measurement and Data (3.MD)			
Solve problems involving measurement and estimation of intervals of time, liquid volumes, and masses of objects.			
Represent and interpret data.			
Geometric measurement: Understand concepts of area, and relate area to multiplication and to addition.			
Geometric measurement: Recognize perimeter as an attribute of plane figures, and distinguish between linear and area measures.			
Geometry (3.G)			
Reason with shapes and their attributes.			
General Comments			

Thus, teacher teams at each grade or course across grades K–12 can use tables similar to table 3.2 (grade 3; page 65) and table 3.3 (high school) to develop a shared understanding of the content, as they review the standards for a particular grade or course and provide their own responses to the analysis questions and compare answers. Visit **go.solution-tree.com/commoncore** for additional analysis tools and online resources from the grade-level books in this series.

Table 3.3: Sample High School Analysis Tool—Geometry

Content Standard Cluster	Which Standards in the Cluster Are Familiar?	What's New or Challenging in These Standards?	Which Standards in the Cluster Need Unpacking or Emphasizing?
Similarity, Right Triangles, and Trigonometry (G-SRT)			
Understand similarity in terms of similarity transformations.			
Prove theorems involving similarity.			
Define trigonometric ratios, and solve problems involving right triangles.			
Apply trigonometry to general triangles.			
General Comments			

Table 3.3 provides the same type of analysis for the high school standard content domain Similarity, Right Triangles, and Trigonometry (G-SRT) in the Geometry conceptual category. Using the four corresponding content standard clusters for this area of the high school standards, the collaborative team answers the understanding questions. This important professional development activity will help teachers better understand the exact expectations of the standards within each cluster and help them to connect to their own prior knowledge and understanding of *what* they are to teach and *how* they are to teach it.

While unpacking each standard is crucial to understanding the intent of the standards, keep in mind that the standards are intentionally grouped within a content standard cluster. Daro, McCallum, and Zimba (2012) emphasize their intentionality (as CCSS for mathematics writers) of the standards within a cluster:

> Fragmenting the Standards into individual standards, or individual bits of standards, erases all these relationships and produces a sum of parts that is decidedly less than the whole. Arranging the Standards into new categories also breaks their structure. It constitutes a remixing of the Standards.

> There is meaning in the cluster headings and domain names that is not contained in the numbered statements beneath them. Remove or reword those headings and you have changed the meaning of the Standards; you now have different Standards; you have not adopted the Common Core. (p. 1)

Thus, in order to address the complex nature of the CCSS for mathematics at the K–12 levels, the work of implementing a CCSS curriculum begins as your curriculum design teams and your collaborative teacher teams work to understand the *learning progressions* aspect of the CCSS that connect the content standards across grade levels.

James Popham (2008) describes a learning progression as a "carefully sequenced set of building blocks that students must master en route to mastering a more distant curricular aim" (p. 84). Learning progressions are a sophisticated way of thinking about big ideas that will reasonably follow one another as students are learning. You can find sample CCSS learning progressions in all the grade-level books for this series and more information about them in the Extending My Understanding section (page 84). The progressions detail why the standards are sequenced the way they are, point out cognitive difficulties students are likely to encounter, provide pedagogical solutions for teachers, and provide more detail on particularly difficult mathematics areas for teachers and students.

Essentially, the learning progressions within the CCSS provide opportunities for teacher teams to see connections between what comes before and after a specific learning target or goal, both in the short term (within a unit) and the long term (across units and across grades). The CCSS for mathematics were built on learning progressions that aim toward the big mathematical ideas of the domains and build in sophistication over time (Confrey, Maloney, & Nguyen, 2010).

At the upper middle school and high school grade levels, course sequencing is a related aspect of the learning progressions. One of the challenges associated with grades 7–12 curriculum design for the CCSS is the inclusion of the content identified as needed "in order to take advanced courses such as calculus, advanced statistics, or discrete mathematics" (NGA & CCSSO, 2010, p. 57). These topics are indicated by a (+) in the high school standards. As students progress through the grades 7–12 curriculum, teachers must pay attention to the development of these standards to ensure that options are open for students to move beyond the standards for college and career readiness. District design teams and the collaborative teams in your PLC should also examine how to design course sequencing within the course scope of standards so that students have ample time to learn the (+) topics as appropriate in grades 7–12.

The progressions, particularly at the elementary level, also illustrate how the development of procedural and conceptual knowledge is intertwined. As the National Research Council (2001) argues in *Adding It Up*:

> The two [procedural fluency and conceptual understanding] are interwoven. Understanding makes learning skills easier, less susceptible to common errors, and less prone to forgetting. By the same token, a certain level of skill is required to learn many mathematical concepts with understanding. (p. 122)

Understanding learning progressions and course sequencing leads to an important aspect of collaborative team planning in mathematics—connecting to student prior knowledge. Making connections to an individual's prior knowledge within a learning progression, such as the grades 3–5 Number and Operations—Fractions domain, significantly influences what is learned in a particular situation (CCSSO, 2008; NRC, 2001, 2009). Thus collaborative teams will need to:

- Write lessons that capitalize on the prior knowledge expected in the CCSS K–12 curriculum

- Write lessons that illustrate an understanding of the learning progressions of that knowledge domain

- Write lessons that include provisions for providing effective formative feedback

- Write lessons at the *depth of student knowledge* that is expected in the CCSS for mathematics

Your role as a school leader is to ensure these content-planning actions are taking place.

Seeking Adequate Time to Teach the Content

As mentioned previously, one of the positive features of the CCSS for mathematics standards is their theme that *less is more*—fewer standards, with more time to teach those important standards deeply. As collaborative teams begin the work of unpacking the content standards, this feature will be revealed. You should know that the CCSS and the assessment of those standards will translate to about a one-third to one-half reduction from the number of typical state standards previously assessed—depending on how the CCSS consortia curricular frameworks unfold.

The caveat is that many of the Common Core standards require teacher-led student activities to drill deeper into the content. The grain size of a unit of instruction is no longer the traditional pace of one standard and one lesson per day. The CCSS require your collaborative teams to shift well beyond one-hundred-plus discrete bodies of knowledge (at a rate of a standard a day) for a grade level or course to a bigger chunk or body of knowledge aimed more at the clusters of standards level—the big ideas of mathematics.

With the CCSS, the idea is to zoom out and think of a grain size of learning built on a complete unit or chapter of study consisting of a cluster of four to six standards lasting three to four weeks. A *unit* now refers to a period of instructional time, not necessarily a discrete unit of mathematics content consisting of eight to ten standards, as has typically been the case. This is because the CCSS mathematics domains are connected in meaningful ways. Your role as a leader is to enable collaborative teams to manage units or clusters of content, instruction, common assessments, and the necessary timely interventions by planning instructional units throughout the year that last three to four weeks.

Figure 3.1 (page 70) shows a sample high school functions unit (or chapter) content and pacing calendar. Such a tool ensures all teachers on the collaborative team plan for the necessary time to teach the content and to ensure all students learn, reflect, and take action on the content for this cluster of standards that are part of the CCSS high school conceptual category Algebra.

Unit 2: Quadratics

Learning target A: Use quadratic functions to model real-world situations (F-IF.4, 5, and 6 and MP 4).

Learning target B: Graph quadratic functions (F-IF.7a).

Learning target C: Write the equation of quadratic functions (F-IF.4).

Learning target D: Solve quadratic equations using factoring, completing the square, or the quadratic formula (A-REI.4b).

Learning target E: Simplify and approximate square roots (A-REI.2).

September				
Monday	Tuesday	Wednesday	Thursday	Friday
				10 02_01: Product of Linears Learning Target A
13 02_02: Quadratic Graphing Learning Target B	14 02_03: Quadratic Graphing Learning Target B	15 02_04: Quadratic Graphic Learning Target B	16 Late Arrival 02_05: Quiz	17 02_06: Quadratic Equation Writing Learning Target C
20 02_07: Quadratic Solving Learning Target D	21 02_08: Quadratic Solving Learning Targets D and E	22 02_09: Quadratic (Formula) Solving Learning Targets D and E	23 02_10: Quadratic (Formula) Solving Learning Targets D and E	24 02_11: Quadratic (Formula) Solving Learning Targets D and E
27 02_12: Quadratic Modeling Learning Target A	28 02_13: Quadratic Modeling Learning Target A	29 02_14: Pretest	30 02_15: Review	1 02_16: Unit 2 Test

Figure 3.1: Sample advanced algebra unit content and pacing calendar for unit 2—quadratics.

Notice in this calendar how twelve days of instruction and four days of assessment are used to unfold the depth of the five standards, or learning targets, for the unit. This collaborative team effectively planned for the time necessary (sixteen days) to ensure student understanding, provide formative feedback to students concerning their progress on the standards' progression in the unit, and provide the time needed to unpack important details of understanding for each learning target from the various clusters the five learning targets represent.

Figure 3.1 is a fairly typical representation of a high school PLC collaborative team calendar. This team could strengthen its current calendar by becoming more explicit about the formative assessment to be used during the content progressions in the unit. Part of your role is to examine the collaborative team calendars that are developed and make sure they meet your expectations for the course content and assessment pacing.

Figure 3.2 shows a sample of how a fourth-grade collaborative team paced its instructional calendar to address four standards under the first two clusters from the CCSS domain Number and Operations in Base Ten (4.NBT). Note that this calendar is more precise in describing fourteen days of mathematics instruction that include the purposeful inclusion of formal formative assessments and planned days for reteaching and enrichment as results of the formative assessments from one unit are connected to the prior knowledge elements of the next unit.

September				
Monday	Tuesday	Wednesday	Thursday	Friday
6 **First day of school:** Orientation activities	7 **Unit 1:** Assess prior knowledge.	8 **Lesson 1:** Model place-value relationships. (NBT.1)	9 **Lesson 2:** Read and write numbers. (NBT.2)	10 **Lesson 3:** Compare and order numbers. (NBT.2)
13 **Lesson 4:** Round numbers. (NBT.3) Midunit formal formative assessment	14 Reteaching and enrichment as indicated by the formative assessment	15 **Lesson 5:** Rename numbers by regrouping. (NBT.1) (NBT.2)	16 **Lesson 6:** Add whole numbers. (NBT.4) (NBT.3) (OA.3)	17 **Lesson 7:** Subtract whole numbers. (NBT.4) (NBT.3) (OA.3)
20 **Lesson 8:** Do comparison problems with addition. (NBT.4)	21 **Lesson 9:** Do comparison problems with subtraction. (NBT.4)	22 Unit 1 assessment	23 Reteaching and enrichment	24 **Unit 2:** Assess prior knowledge. Start lesson 1.

Figure 3.2: Grade 4 pacing calendar for unit 1—place value, addition, and subtraction to one million.

If the fourth-grade collaborative team in this example works together to provide all students with additional support, then specific team members can take different groups of students who may need reteaching and re-engagement of particular topics. Those team members can provide additional instructional support, while another team member can provide enrichment and extension activities for students who have demonstrated proficiency. Finally, it is also worth noting that like the sixteen days for unit 2 in the high school calendar, these fourteen days are not simply one standard per day. Individual standards are covered on multiple days, and individual lessons may include multiple standards emphasizing the connected nature of the CCSS content standards and the focus on big mathematical ideas.

As a school leader, you will want to ensure your local curricular frameworks align with your state's standard assessment consortia frameworks. The Partnership for Assessment of Readiness for College and Careers (PARCC) and the SMARTER Balanced Assessment Consortium (SBAC) represent the two testing and assessment consortia for the CCSS. Each consortium has developed content frameworks for grades 3–11 that provide guidance on how and when to implement the standards during the course of a school year. These frameworks provide support for your work at the local school site and district level. (You should check your state website or visit www.parcconline.org /about-parcc or www.smarterbalanced.org for the latest information about the assessment consortia progress.)

These websites provide sample instructional units, sample assessment tasks, professional development modules, and classroom resources. Your curriculum design teams can use the information from the frameworks to set priorities for grade-level content emphasis, unit development, and organization of content units. Be sure that careful attention is given to the content focus and emphasis of these frameworks. You will want to make sure that units of instruction and the emphasis taught in your school or district are aligned with the framework appropriate to your state's assessment consortia.

Accessing Appropriate Technology and Strategic Tools

NCTM (2008c), in its technology position statement, states, "Leaders and teachers take responsibility for the systemic classroom integration of effective technologies to enhance the curriculum, pedagogy, assessments and approaches to equity" (p. 1). When used effectively, technology can be a powerful instructional tool (Battista, 2008; Zbiek, 2010). The CCSS Mathematical Practices require students to develop mathematical models and use appropriate tools (NGA & CCSSO, 2010) as discussed in chapter 2. Your job is to ensure that each collaborative team develops and implements a plan for the effective use of technology as a way to engage students in the Mathematical Practices. The question is not whether or not to use technology. The question is, How well will your teams integrate technology in a way that supports learning for each student around the content standards?

With today's 21st century digital tools, teachers need to develop student discernment regarding which tool a student should access. For example, students can view multiple answers for a mathematical problem at many websites, such as www.wolframalpha.com, or through interactive algebra, geometry, or statistics apps. However, students also need to demonstrate how they interpret answers, understand the reasonableness of solutions, and make sense of those solutions and arguments regardless of the technology used to support their thinking.

Stacey and Wiliam (in press) point out that the increasing sophistication and power of technology will support the work of your collaborative teams to engage students in tasks in different ways, and "ensure that students adhere to constraints imposed on solutions." NCSM (2011), in *Improving Student Achievement in Mathematics by Systematically Integrating Effective Technology*, identifies four ways to integrate research-affirmed technology practices with teaching and learning practices:

1. Increase student interactivity with content.

2. Connect multiple representations for differentiation of content development.

3. Increase student-to-student collaboration and discussion.

4. Collect and organize feedback for students and teachers on formative assessment processes (discussed and developed in chapter 4).

To build conceptual knowledge, students need opportunities to interact with mathematics and digital tools that can deliver this type of instruction and feedback to students. Your collaborative teams need to account for the influence of technology in the unit-by-unit teaching and learning of mathematics—including embracing CCSS Mathematical Practice 5, Use appropriate tools strategically.

Your teacher teams will need to purposefully plan how to *integrate* specific technologies to reach all students as they develop new content units for the CCSS. When teachers plan a unit of instruction and the common mathematical tasks, you should help teachers identify which technological tool (graphing calculator, tablet computer applications, web 2.0 tools, interactive games, blogs, adaptive test generators, and so on) will assist them in making the mathematics more meaningful. Once you identify the tool, teams need to articulate the purpose of the tool and how it will complement the expected student learning outcomes. Once agreed, all team members must allow their students the benefit of the technology as they use tools that will also serve the expectations of student performance on the CCSS consortia assessments.

As a leader, it is your responsibility to ensure that your elementary teams in particular, and teams at all levels, have access to a variety of mathematical tools to support their students' mathematical explorations. These explorations may occur with concrete manipulatives (such as base-ten blocks, color tiles, pattern blocks, cubes, fraction tiles, two-color counters, and number cubes) or with virtual manipulatives. Finding the necessary resources to obtain these tools may be one of the priorities you set as a leader.

It is also critical that you monitor your elementary teams to ensure their collaboratively developed lesson plans provide students with instruction in selecting appropriate tools for a particular student mathematics exploration of a content standard. It is important to keep in mind that often a mathematical tool can be used instructionally in multiple areas of mathematics. For instance, a set of pattern blocks is useful not only for studying numerical and visual patterns but also for studying fractions and geometry (models for plane figures and symmetry). Sometimes students may be uncertain about which tool to use for a particular mathematical task. When teachers provide guidance instead of selecting tools for students, they provide space for students to make hypotheses, try new ways of studying mathematics, and have a context for comparing how different tools can either be useful or a hindrance for studying the specific mathematics. Here are five questions your collaborative teams can use to help students select the most appropriate tool for working on a mathematics task (Larson et al., 2012):

1. Does the tool provide a meaningful model to support the mathematics?

2. Does the tool extend students' thinking and support their learning of the given mathematical topic?

3. Is the tool necessary?

4. Is the tool easy to use?

5. Does the tool provide support for students to engage in and solve a problem?

Teachers may find that it is very engaging (and even enjoyable) to teach mathematics with a variety of tools. However, the real issue is whether student learning is supported by the use of tools. Tools such as manipulatives or technology should not be used simply for the sake of using them. Monitoring your teams' appropriate use of tools to ensure that they are truly used strategically is a critical role for you as a leader and a way you can support the implementation of the Mathematical Practices.

Implementing the CCSS Content Standards

Ultimately, a major aspect of your school leadership role is to ensure the CCSS are implemented in classrooms as intended. The CCSS delineate and define the expectations but do not indicate exactly how to prepare and implement the teaching and learning of those standards.

The following collaborative team strategies will help ensure all teachers implement the identified CCSS. On a unit-by-unit basis, teachers and teacher teams should have:

- Clearly articulated learning targets

- Specified teaching strategies for those learning targets

- Identified common unit tasks

- Common in-class formative assessment instruments and tools that provide feedback to students and monitor progress individually and collectively toward the learning targets

These four collaborative strategies are the basis for collaborative strategies you can use with your teams to enable teachers to provide feedback to students and monitor progress individually and collectively toward the learning targets.

During instructional planning for a unit of content, teacher teams must be attentive to what the student *will learn* (the learning target) as well as what the student *will do* (the learning activity or task and how the task results will be assessed). As teachers and teacher teams plan for instruction, the learning goals for the unit are identified first, and then the appropriate sequence of tasks and student experiences teachers will use to enable students to meet the goal is decided. Consequently, student learning is driven by mastery of the learning goals, and the tasks and activities are chosen to help support student learning progressions and the formative assessment of that learning through the unit. Thus the work of the collaborative team, on a unit-by-unit basis, begins with identifying the learning targets.

Collaborative Strategy One: Clearly Articulated Learning Targets

Your CCSS for mathematics curriculum must identify the specific learning targets (standards) that are expected of students at each grade level or course. As your collaborative teams develop unit-by-unit or chapter-by-chapter learning targets, attention must be paid to the *depth of knowledge* that each target will require

Stein et al. (2009) define the cognitive demand of a task as "the kind and level of thinking required of students in order to successfully engage with and solve a task" (p. 1). They further identify low-level-cognitive-demand tasks as memorizing or applying procedures without connections. High-level-cognitive-demand tasks are procedures with connections or what the authors call *doing mathematics*, whereby students engage in more complex reasoning, analyzing, and problem solving. The learning target of the lesson dictates the cognitive level of task. If the learning target is for students to develop fluency, low-level-cognitive-demand tasks are appropriate. However, if students only work through tasks of low-level cognitive demand, they do not develop the connected and deep mathematical understanding needed to apply their knowledge in new situations. As Stein et al. (2009) state, "Students also need opportunities on a regular basis to engage with tasks that lead to deeper, more generative understandings regarding the nature of mathematical processes, concepts, and relationships" (p. 5).

When students engage in high-cognitive-demand tasks the teacher team selects to connect to and build on to prior student knowledge, the students become involved in thinking critically, reasoning mathematically, and making sense of what they are learning about the knowledge they are acquiring. Tasks that have multiple entry points and can be solved in multiple ways not only result in richer student discourse but also allow all students access to the mathematics. Webb (1997) provides more information on high-cognitive-demand task development. He identifies four levels to describe the depth of knowledge (DOK) required by learning targets: (1) recall, (2) skill and concept,

(3) strategic thinking, and (4) extended thinking. (You can visit http://facstaff.wcer.wisc
.edu/normw for the descriptions of each of the four DOK levels. Visit **go.solution-tree
.com/commoncore** for a link to this resource.)

Since the CCSS curriculum should address learning at all depths of knowledge, table
3.4 highlights an example of a concept unit from first-year algebra and its connections
to five specific CCSS high school content standards across two conceptual categories—
Number and Quantity (Quantities [N-Q] content standard cluster) and Algebra (Seeing
Structure in Expressions [A-SSE] and Creating Equations [A-CED] content standard
clusters). Table 3.5 provides a similar example for grade 2.

Table 3.4: Sample Algebra Unit on Equations and Inequalities

CCSS Standard	CCSS Standard Description	Student-Friendly Learning Target (Derived From Unpacking the Standards)	Technology Expectations
N-Q.1	Use units as a way to understand problems and to guide the solution of multistep problems; choose and interpret units consistently in formulas; choose and interpret the scale and the origin in graphs and data displays.	I can use units (centimeters, seconds, grams, and so on) appropriately through the problem-solving process. I can understand units that are used in graphical displays.	• Use a graphing calculator to solve a single-variable equation by setting each side equal to y. • Use a graphing calculator to explore algebraic structure and equivalence. • Manipulate the settings of the calculator to show answers to the appropriate level of accuracy, including scientific notation. • Graph a linear equation and analyze for solutions to real-world problems.
N-Q.2	Define appropriate quantities for the purpose of descriptive modeling.	I can identify the correct type of measurement to represent a real-life situation.	
N-Q.3	Choose a level of accuracy appropriate to limitations on measurement when reporting quantities.	I can estimate to an appropriate level of accuracy.	
A-SSE.1	Interpret expressions that represent a quantity in terms of its context.★ a. Interpret parts of an expression, such as terms, factors, and coefficients.	I can understand the vocabulary of the parts of an algebraic expression. I can understand the meaning of algebraic structure.	

CCSS Standard	CCSS Standard Description	Student-Friendly Learning Target (Derived From Unpacking the Standards)	Technology Expectations
A-SSE.1 (continued)	b. Interpret complicated expressions by viewing one or more of their parts as a single entity. For example, interpret $P(1 + r)n$ as the product of P and a factor not depending on P.		
A-CED.1	Create equations and inequalities in one variable and use them to solve problems. Include equations arising from linear and quadratic functions and simple rational and exponential functions. (Limit functions to linear, quadratic, and exponential with integer inputs only.)	I can set up an equation to solve a real-world problem with one unknown variable. I can solve the equation to find the answer to the real-world problem.	

Note: Notice that A-SSE.1 is a starred item. In the high school standards, a star indicates that the specific focus of the standard is the mathematical modeling aspect of the standard.

Table 3.5: Sample Grade 2 Unit on Two-Digit Subtraction

CCSS Standard	CCSS Standard Description	Student-Friendly Learning Target (Derived From Unpacking the Standards)	Technology Expectations
NBT.5	Fluently add and subtract within 100 using strategies based on place value, properties of operations, or the relationship between addition and subtraction.	I can subtract two two-digit numbers. I can use addition to find differences.	• Dry-erase marker boards • Base-ten blocks • Ten-frames • Interlocking cubes

continued →

CCSS Standard	CCSS Standard Description	Student-Friendly Learning Target (Derived From Unpacking the Standards)	Technology Expectations
NBT.9	Explain why addition and subtraction strategies work, using place value and the properties of operations.	I can explain my thinking when I subtract two two-digit numbers using a drawing or base-ten blocks.	• Dry-erase marker boards • Base-ten blocks • Ten-frames • Interlocking cubes
OA.1	Use addition and subtraction within 100 to solve one- and two-step word problems involving situations of adding to, taking from, putting together, taking apart, and comparing, with unknowns in all positions—for example, by using drawings and equations with a symbol for the unknown number to represent the problem.	I can solve a word problem that requires two-digit subtraction by drawing a picture.	• Dry-erase marker boards • Base-ten blocks • Ten-frames • Interlocking cubes

Notice in the high school example in table 3.4 (page 76), there are only five Common Core standards for the concept unit on equations and inequalities. This reflects the focused nature of the CCSS standards and the depth of teaching and learning expected in a unit of the curriculum that may take as many as fourteen to sixteen days to unwrap for the students. In the grade 2 example (table 3.5), the unit will require much more than three lessons (one lesson per day) to ensure the level of student proficiency the CCSS require (as any second-grade teacher knows). Notice too that the Common Core standards are rewritten into student-friendly language that will be used during and after the unit for students to identify the learning targets they either do know or do not know (and thus need to work on more throughout the unit). This language is designed to foster greater student ownership of the learning targets for the unit.

The next natural step in the collaborative team planning process once the learning targets are decided and the level of cognitive demand for the tasks used to teach and learn the learning targets are in place is to determine the teaching strategies and Mathematical Practices that will be used and emphasized during the unit.

Collaborative Strategy Two: Specified Teaching Strategies

Another required part of the identified CCSS curriculum will be the specific teaching strategies that may be used to elicit the desired level of learning. When your collaborative teams identify the unit learning targets, such as those in table 3.6 (page 80) or table 3.7 (page 81), they should also identify the teaching strategies that will result in student development of the CCSS Mathematical Practices from chapter 2. Without the connected teaching strategies that support the content standards, your teacher teams are left without the guidance needed to support meaningful student learning for understanding. While individual teachers may be able to design lessons with a stated target in mind, in order for the curriculum teams to engage in the collective inquiry that is expected in a professional learning community, a set of identified teaching strategies representative of the eight CCSS Mathematical Practices will help to exemplify the student understanding and the desired learning of the content standard. As a leader, your role is to help the teacher teams reach agreement on the teaching strategies they will use.

Consider the verbs used with many of the CCSS content standards (learning targets and goals for the unit). These verbs for student action are *interpret* the expression, *understand* the parts of vocabulary, *understand* problems, or *choose* a level of accuracy. These action verbs each require various teaching strategies that reflect the CCSS Mathematical Practices. Designing these strategies, as part of the content discussion, becomes the real work of your collaborative teams—the very teams shouldered with the primary responsibility of CCSS K–12 mathematics implementation.

Collaborative Strategy Three: Identified Common Unit Tasks

As students progress through a curriculum, they should learn mathematics by engaging in "worthwhile mathematical tasks" (Hiebert et al., 2003) and by engaging in discourse expertly orchestrated by the teacher (Chapin & O'Connor, 2007; Smith & Stein, 2011). The common grade-level or course-based unit tasks in which students engage provide the common experiences that can be drawn on to further learning at various points throughout the curriculum. In many districts, it is the identified common mathematical tasks (selected during the unit planning process) that provide teachers the opportunity for collaborative discussions regarding student performance. That is, the identified common tasks in a curriculum provide important points of departure for conversations about student learning. When your collaborative teams can immerse themselves in examples of student work and both qualitative and quantitative data from those common experiences, the team can identify an instructional focus for continued student growth and improve the learning for all students at a particular grade level or in a particular course.

Table 3.6 (page 80) and table 3.7 (page 81) provide examples of a district design team's developed unit of study. For collaborative teams in a PLC, the team members must select the nature of the tasks to be used (the cognitive demand) for each standard or learning target. This selection may come from current instructional materials for the mathematics program or may come from outside resources for public-domain tasks. All team members should use common mathematical tasks with the necessary depth and rigor to ensure equitable opportunity for student learning of the expected CCSS content standards. Thus, you can use tables 3.6 and 3.7 as templates, or guides, to help teachers and teacher teams learn how to connect the CCSS learning targets to identified and specified teaching strategies, core high-cognitive-demand tasks, and common formative classroom assessments that provide feedback to students and monitor progress individually and collectively toward the learning targets.

Table 3.6: PLC Design Questions for Standard Implementation—Fourth-Grade Number and Operations—Fractions Example

Learning Target (What Students Will Be Able to Do)	Teaching Strategies (Approaches Teachers Will Use)	Common Tasks (Tasks All Students Will Use)	Common Formative Assessment (Points to Guide Teacher Feedback to Students)
Understand that to add or subtract fractions they must refer to parts of the same whole.	Cooperative learning investigation followed by whole-class discussion	Students will use fraction bars and a number line with colored pencils to build fractions from unit fractions.	Do all students know when they can add or subtract parts of a whole?
Decompose a fraction by writing it as a sum of fractions with the same denominators.	Student pairs using tasks provided in curricular materials followed by whole-class discussion	Students will use fraction bars and number lines to investigate.	Can all students write a fraction as a sum of fractions with the same denominator?
Use models to represent and find sums involving fractions.	Cooperative learning investigation followed by whole-class instruction	Students will use pictures, fraction bars, and number lines to investigate fraction addition.	Can all students add fractions with like denominators using models?
Use models to represent and find differences involving fractions.	Cooperative learning investigation followed by whole-class instruction	Students will use pictures, fraction bars, number lines, and area models to investigate fraction subtraction.	Can all students subtract fractions with unlike denominators using models?
Solve word problems involving addition and subtraction with fractions.	Applied problem-solving situations	Students will solve a variety of applied problems using the district's online fourth-grade math materials folder.	Can students model and solve one-step applied problem situations using fractions?

Visit **go.solution-tree.com/commoncore** for a reproducible version of this table.

Table 3.7: PLC Design Questions for Standard Implementation—High School Example

Learning Target (What Students Will Be Able to Do)	Teaching Strategies (Approaches Teachers Will Use)	Common Tasks (Tasks All Students Will Use)	Common Formative Assessment (Points to Guide Teacher Feedback to Students)
State the properties of a dilation given by a center and a scale factor (G-SRT.1).	Cooperative learning exploration and reporting out	Students will participate in a dilation lab to explore the properties of dilations.	Can all students state the properties in writing and to their peers?
Verify the properties experimentally (G-SRT.2).	Hand-drawn triangles and dynamic geometry software	Teachers use the problems from the electronic file in the district's geometry materials folder.	Can the student verify the properties in other settings?
Determine if two triangles are similar (G-SRT.3).	Triangle lab in small groups	Students should construct similar triangles using a pencil and paper and dynamic geometry software.	Can students correctly identify proportional relationships after identifying two triangles as similar?
State and use the angle-angle similarity criterion (G-SRT.3).	Experiments with similar triangles	Students should construct similar triangles using a pencil and paper and dynamic geometry software.	Can students correctly identify proportional relationships after identifying two triangles as similar?
Prove the theorems in the Similarity, Right Triangles, and Trigonometry domain (G-SRT.4).	Cooperative learning with some whole-class guidance	Teachers use resource 5 from unit materials that the district math team developed for this unit.	Students will prove the theorems. Can students work in pairs to explain and justify the theorems regarding triangle similarity, highlighting necessary steps and validating their reasons with precise language?
Solve problems using similarity (G-SRT.6).	Small-group practice	Teachers use the problems from the level 3 cognitive-demand online work folder	Can students understand the logical path for solving the problems?

continued →

Learning Target (What Students Will Be Able to Do)	Teaching Strategies (Approaches Teachers Will Use)	Common Tasks (Tasks All Students Will Use)	Common Formative Assessment (Points to Guide Teacher Feedback to Students)
Explain the relationship between sine and cosine of complementary angles (G-SRT.7).	Students in pairs (such as quiz-quiz-trade)	Students will participate in trigonometry lab 2 provided in the district materials for this unit.	Can students state the relationship and justify their reasoning?
Identify the trigonometric ratios in right triangles (G-SRT.8).	Students in pairs (such as quiz-quiz-trade)	Students will participate in trigonometry lab 1 provided in the district materials for this unit.	Can students demonstrate to their peers the relationship between sine, cosine, and similar triangles?
Use trigonometric ratios with the Pythagorean theorem to solve triangles (G-SRT.8).	Applied problem-solving situations	Students will participate in trigonometry lab 3 from our team folder for the unit.	Can students solve one- and multiple-step problems?

Visit **go.solution-tree.com/commoncore** for a reproducible version of this table.

Collaborative Strategy Four: Common In-Class Formative Assessment

In addition to identified common unit tasks, you can lead the collaborative team to actively seek data that pertain to agreed-on checkpoints for student understanding. As the team discusses the learning targets for an upcoming unit, you should also help them reach agreement on how to assess that learning. Then, as team members design their lessons for that unit, you can guide them in identifying the common points of in-class formative assessment processes that will be used to gather data to provide feedback to students and to the team.

These embedded in-class formative assessment opportunities are a natural outgrowth of the discussions within the collaborative teamwork and allow for immediate feedback for both students and teachers as part of the common tasks. Without these common in-class formative moments the team members do not have the information they need to know whether or not all students are learning and understanding at the desired level. As described in chapter 2, using figure 2.12 (page 53), you can assist the team to prepare both the *advancing* (enhancing concepts beyond the common task) and the *assessing* (scaffolding the concept for differentiation) formative questions to be used by the teachers and students during the in-class activities designed for the task. We have included examples of formative assessment points in table 3.6 (page 80) and table 3.7 in order to help teachers on the team identify whether students are learning the standard's expectations. Chapter 4 will examine in much more detail exactly how to provide this type of feedback.

Looking Ahead

This chapter was intended to help you focus the work of your collaborative teams as they begin content discussions regarding the CCSS expectations as part of your curriculum redesign effort. Teachers participating in collaborative teams must decide for themselves, under your leadership, the depth desired (or needed) for such content knowledge development and analysis. The grade-level books that accompany this series can help with that analysis in much greater detail.

The recommendations and tools in this chapter can guide your school's professional development efforts in thinking about, analyzing, and unpacking the domains and clusters for the K–12 CCSS mathematics expectations. It will be the responsibility of the district curriculum design teams as well as your school site collaborative teams to implement the vision for the Common Core State Standards and, as the next chapter will suggest, the assessment of those standards.

Chapter 3 Extending My Understanding

1. Observe a collaborative team as it examines a specific CCSS domain.

   o How do the standards and clusters within this specific domain develop over a student's grade band (K–2, 3–5, 6–8, or high school) experience? Refer to table 3.6 (page 80) for an example.

   o How do teachers respond as they conduct a side-by-side comparison of the CCSS with your current mathematics curriculum standards spending time unpacking and looking for emphasis? Refer to the table 3.4 (page 76) for an example.

   o How does the collaborative team identify the familiar, new, or challenging content? How might this impact your support of its content implementation plan?

2. Observe a collaborative team as it examines a specific CCSS cluster.

   o What are the specific learning targets that are expected of students at each level of curriculum? Refer to table 3.7 (page 81).

   o What mathematical tasks could be used to develop student understanding of the standards within this cluster?

   o What Mathematical Practices are developed within this specific cluster of standards?

3. Work with your collaborative teams to examine the instructional materials currently used to support your mathematics curriculum. Determine the extent to which these materials are aligned with the CCSS by using the Mathematics

Curriculum Materials Analysis Project tools discussed in the online resources. How will you use this information to guide planning, delivery of instruction, and effective assessment?

Online Resources

Visit **go.solution-tree.com/commoncore** for links to these resources. Visit www.core standards.org/assets/CCSSI_Math%20Standards.pdf to view the Common Core State Standards for mathematics (NGA & CCSSO, 2010).

- **CCSS Mathematics Curriculum Materials Analysis Project (Bush et al., 2011; www.mathedleadership.org/docs/ccss/CCSSO%20Mathematics%20 Curriculum%20Analysis%20Project.Whole%20Document.6.1.11.Final .docx):** The CCSS Mathematics Curriculum Analysis Project provides a set of tools to assist K–12 textbook selection committees, school administrators, and teachers in the analysis and selection of curriculum materials that support implementation of the CCSS for mathematics.

- **Illustrative Mathematics Project (http://illustrativemathematics.org):** The main goal for this project is to provide guidance to states, assessment consortia, testing companies, and curriculum developers by illustrating the range and types of mathematical work that students will experience in implementing the Common Core State Standards for mathematics.

- **Progressions Documents for the Common Core Mathematics Standards (Institute for Mathematics and Education, 2007; http://math.arizona.edu /~ime/progressions):** The CCSS for mathematics were built on progressions— narrative documents describing the progression of a topic across a number of grade levels, informed both by research on children's cognitive development and by the logical structure of mathematics. The progressions detail why standards are sequenced the way they are, point out cognitive difficulties and provide pedagogical solutions, and provide more detail on particularly difficult areas of mathematics. The progressions documents found here are useful in teacher preparation, professional development, and curriculum organization, and they provide a link between mathematics education research and the standards.

- **Recommendations for CCSS Professional Development (http://commoncore tools.files.wordpress.com/2011/05/2011_04_27_gearing_up.pdf):** These initial recommendations are from the Gearing Up for the Common Core State Standards in Mathematics conference. They can serve as guidelines for K–8 mathematics professional development for states transitioning to the CCSS.

- **Livescribe Pencasts (www.livescribe.com):** You may want to consider using pencasts of student work to help drive collaborative discussions related to student understanding of important standards within each of the content domains for grades K–12.

CHAPTER 4

Leading the Implementation of the Teaching-Assessing-Learning Cycle

An assessment functions formatively to the extent that evidence about student achievement is elicited, interpreted, and used by teachers, learners, or their peers to make decisions about the next steps in instruction that are likely to be better, or better founded, than the decisions they would have made in absence of that evidence.

—Dylan Wiliam

The focus of this chapter is to illustrate the appropriate use of ongoing student assessment as part of an interactive, cyclical, and systemic collaborative team *formative process* on a unit-by-unit basis. You can support your collaborative teams by using this chapter as the engine that will drive your systematic development for student attainment of the Common Core mathematics content and instruction described in chapters 2 and 3.

When led well, ongoing unit-by-unit mathematics assessments—whether in class, during the lesson checks or end-of-unit assessment instruments, like tests, quizzes, or projects—serve as a feedback bridge within the teaching-assessing-learning cycle. The cycle requires your teams to identify core learning targets or standards for the unit, create cognitively demanding common mathematics tasks that reflect the learning targets, create in-class formative assessments of those targets, and design common assessment instruments to be used during and at the end of a unit of instruction.

To embrace the student assessment and learning expectations within the Common Core, your teacher teams will constantly need to collect evidence of student learning and respond to that evidence (decide and *act* on what to do next) using rich, descriptive, and immediate corrective feedback as part of a formative decision-making process.

You can use this chapter to help your teacher teams systematically support student attainment of the CCSS for mathematics in your school and district. Assessment can no longer solely serve a summative function for teachers—that of assigning grades and providing accountability—if the goal is to motivate and improve student learning and to successfully implement the CCSS. For mathematics teaching and learning to improve, the formative assessment process becomes an intense focus of the collaborative team. Your leadership can enable teams to make this change from assessment as an ends to assessment as a means to support and advance student learning.

A Paradigm Shift in K–12 Mathematics Assessment Practices

Think about the current assessment practices and processes your collaborative teams and others in your mathematics program use. What are they like? How would you know with any certainty if those assessment practices are of high quality and represent a process that will significantly impact student achievement?

Student assessment has largely been considered an isolated teacher activity that served the primary summative purpose of grading. Thus, assessment instruments (mostly quizzes, tests, and projects) primarily serve as an *ends*, not as a *means* to support and advance student learning. Generally, when used as an end, assessment instruments do not result in student motivation to persevere (Mathematical Practice 1) and continue learning.

If teachers use each quiz, test, or chapter assessment instrument as a summative evaluation moment for the student, often there is little, if any, opportunity for the student to take action and respond to the evidence of learning the assessment provides. In this limited vision of how teachers use assessment instruments (as an ends), each teacher would give a quiz or test to the students, privately grade the test answers as right or wrong—based on a personal scoring rubric determined in isolation from other colleagues—and then pass back student scores (grades) for the test and for the current class grade.

The teacher returns the assessment instrument to his or her students, who in turn either file away the test or turn it back in. Typically, teachers file away the results and move on to the next chapter or unit of teaching—while also responding to the students who failed to take the test on time. For the most part, student learning on the previous unit stopped at this point because the unit ended. Do any of these isolated assessment practices seem familiar in your school or district?

Now, with the Common Core State Standards for mathematics, the fundamental purpose and process for the ongoing unit-by-unit student assessment in mathematics is undergoing a significant change. In a professional learning community, mathematics assessment functions as a multifaceted, evidence-collecting team process by which teachers gather information about student learning and teacher practice in order to inform teacher *and* student daily decision making, and to adjust the focus of instruction and learning accordingly. For student mathematics learning to improve according to the CCSS, teachers will need to shift their assessment work from (1) preparing for external summative assessments used for accountability and (2) creating summative assessment instruments strictly to assign grades, to using *formative assessment* processes that continuously improve instruction and student learning.

Figure 4.1 lists the critical questions collaborative teams should consider to begin the process of implementing formative assessment in a planned way. Your leadership role is to ensure each team addresses these questions as you help them to gain insight into their understanding of assessment practices that bridge the gap between their teaching and evidence of student learning.

1. In advance of teaching the lesson, chapter, and unit of study (all three levels of plan-ning), how well does each member of the collaborative team understand the stu-dent learning targets (content standard, depth of knowledge, and Mathematical Practices) and the assessments aligned with those learning targets?

2. Has the team collaboratively developed and agreed on scoring rubrics and proce-dures, for both formative and summative assessment instruments, that will accu-rately reflect student achievement of the learning targets?

3. To what degree do the collaborative team's assessments build student confidence and encourage students to take responsibility for what they know and still have to learn?

4. How well does the collaborative team provide timely formative assessment feed-back that is both frequent and descriptive (versus summative and evaluative), pro-viding students with specific information regarding their strengths as well as strate-gies to improve?

5. How well does each member of the collaborative team, and the team as a collective group, modify instruction or provide additional instructional supports for students as necessary, based on the results of both formative and summative classroom assessment to improve student learning and future instruction?

Source: Adapted from Kanold et al., 2012.

Figure 4.1: Key assessment questions for collaborative teams.

Visit **go.solution-tree.com/commoncore** for a reproducible version of this figure.

When you address these key questions with your collaborative teams, you provide the support they need in shifting the assessment emphasis from one that views assessment as primarily something that occurs at the end of instruction to determine if learning has occurred to an ongoing formative process that is used to improve teaching and learning.

Collaborative teams use robust assessment processes grounded in the ongoing retrieval and analysis of information about the depth and rigor of student tasks, the effective learning of those mathematical tasks, and the creation of a learning environment where "error is welcomed as a learning opportunity, where discarding incorrect knowledge and understandings is welcomed, and where participants [teachers and students] can feel safe to learn, re-learn, and explore knowledge and understanding" (Hattie, 2009, p. 239). In this new paradigm, the appropriate use of ongoing student assessment becomes part of an interactive, cyclical, and systemic collaborative team *formative process.*

James Popham (2011a) makes the case for a formative assessment process that gathers evidence in a variety of ways moving from "traditional written tests to a wide range of informal assessment procedures" (p. 36):

> Recent reviews of more than 4000 research investigations show clearly that when the [formative assessment] process is well implemented in the classroom, it can essentially double the speed of student learning produc-ing large gains in students' achievement, and at the same time, it is suf-ficiently robust so different teachers can use it in diverse ways and still get great results with their students. (Popham, 2011a, p. 36)

As a school leader, ensuring your collaborative teams implement formative assessment processes is a key responsibility. In this new paradigm, collaborative teams understand that school mathematics assessments are no longer driven by and limited to the traditional *summative* purpose of using unit or chapter tests and quizzes, districtwide benchmark tests, semester final exams, and high-stakes state or national assessments to assign grades, scores, and rankings. A new expectation is evident—that your teacher teams will use the *assessment instruments and the information from them* to make improvements and adjustments to their instruction and techniques for student learning. Essentially, any traditional school assessment instrument used for a grading purpose is only one part of a much bigger, multistep formative process necessary for teacher and student learning (Popham, 2008).

In this era of CCSS, formative assessment practices now take precedence. Locally developed collaborative team tests and quizzes, semester final exams, and district benchmark exams will be embraced as *assessment instruments* that serve the priority formative purpose in which error is welcomed as a learning opportunity for teachers and students alike. Together, you and your school collaborative teams will plan for and collaborate on ways in which the locally developed unit or chapter quizzes, tests, and benchmark exams are to be used primarily to help students self-assess their own understanding for improvement and then act as necessary to improve.

It is important that your collaborative teams understand that formative assessment is not a type of test administered to students. Popham (2011a) provides a great analogy to describe the difference between summative assessment *instruments* and formative assessment *processes*. He describes the difference between a surfboard and surfing. While a surfboard represents an important tool in surfing, it is only that—a part of the surfing process. The entire process involves the surfer paddling out to an appropriate offshore location, selecting the right wave, choosing the most propitious moment to catch the chosen wave, standing upright on the surfboard, and staying upright while a curling wave rumbles toward shore. The surfboard is a key component of the surfing process, but it is not the entire process.

High-quality school assessment practices then function to integrate formative assessment processes into the teacher's decisive actions about shaping instruction to meet student needs—progress, pacing, and next steps. Similarly, these processes inform students about their learning progress and direction, enabling them to become actively involved and to take ownership of their work. Teachers learn more about their instructional practice and students learn more about how to focus the re-engagement of their learning by:

1. Using unit-by-unit assessment instruments such as quizzes, projects, and tests as tools to support a formative learning process for teachers and students (steps one, four, and five of the assessment cycle)

2. Designing and implementing in-class formative assessment strategies and advancing and assessing questions that check for student understanding during the classroom period (steps two and three of the assessment cycle)

Wiliam's (2011) epigraph at the start of this chapter reveals the definition of *formative assessment* used in this book:

> An assessment functions formatively to the extent that evidence about student achievement is elicited, interpreted, and used by teachers, learners, or their peers to make decisions about the next steps in instruction that are likely to be better, or better founded, than the decisions they would have made in absence of that evidence. (p. 43)

There are two key phrases in Wiliam's definition: (1) "evidence about student achievement is elicited" and (2) "[assessment functions to] make decisions about next steps." That is, teacher and students in conjunction with their peers must *act* on the evidence. Otherwise, as Wiliam (2011) describes, the formative process is empty in terms of impact on student learning.

Furthermore, Wiliam (2011) cites five elements that need to be in place if the intent of teaching and assessing during the lesson (the daily choice of mathematical tasks teachers use for short-cycle assessments and checks for understanding) and unit (teachers' weekly or monthly choice of assessment instruments such as quizzes and tests) is to improve student learning. You can use these elements as a basis for monitoring the quality of your teacher teams' current formative assessment practices. The five elements are:

1. The provision of effective and timely feedback to students

2. The active involvement of students in their own learning

3. The adjustment of teaching to take into account the results of assessment

4. The recognition of the profound influence assessment has on the motivation and self-esteem of students, both of which are crucial to learning

5. The need for students to be able to assess themselves and understand how to improve

The teaching-assessing-learning cycle is built on the expectations of these essential assessment elements. The cycle is designed to develop a vision of effective high-quality assessment practices on a unit-by-unit basis for the teachers in your mathematics program. Your teams work together to determine how to provide students with formative learning opportunities and equitable strategies on learning targets as teachers respond to evidence (or lack thereof) of student learning.

The PLC Teaching-Assessing-Learning Cycle

The PLC teaching-assessing-learning cycle described in figure 4.2 (page 90) provides a systemic collaborative team process that will recognize any assessments used—from the daily in-class informal checks for understanding with student feedback, to the more formal unit assessment instruments—as formative, provided teachers and students use them to make instructional and learning adjustments. In your professional development efforts, communicate and support the use of the assessment cycle to teachers to sustain a focused and coherent instruction and content implementation. When you help teachers and teacher teams use assessment instruments as tools within a robust team assessment

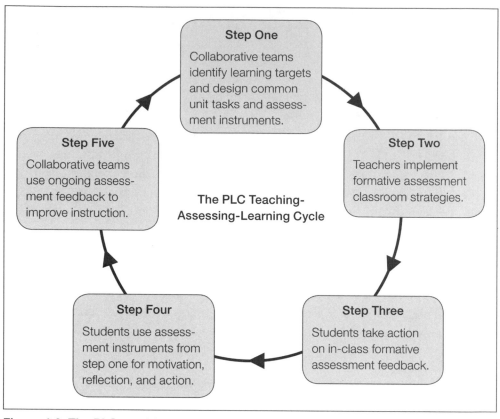

Figure 4.2: The PLC teaching-assessing-learning cycle.

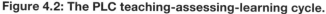

Visit **go.solution-tree.com/commoncore** for a reproducible version of this figure.

plan and process cycle, great things can happen. When in-class formative feedback is part of your teams' lesson design, and planning and teaching become "*adaptive* to student learning needs" (Wiliam & Thompson, 2008, p. 64), you can expect to see marked improvement in student achievement.

Moving clockwise in figure 4.2, your collaborative teacher teams make adjustments and move back and forth in the cycle as needed, giving feedback to students and to each other. In step one, the teachers do the hard work of planning for the unit—for the learning targets, the common and essential mathematical tasks, the formative response to in-class tasks, and the design of the common assessment instruments to use throughout the unit. In steps two and three, teachers use daily formative assessment classroom strategies around the team-designed mathematical tasks from step one and make adjustments as needed during the unit.

In step four, teachers establish processes in which students set goals and make adjustments to learning based on all unit or chapter assessment instrument results at a developmentally appropriate level depending on the grade level. (This will seem different from the primary grades to high school courses.) Students are required by teachers to reflect on successes and to take next-step actions based on evidence of areas of failure *during* and *after* the unit of study.

Ultimately, in step five, teachers make adjustments to future lesson plans and unit assessment instruments due to individual differences in students and the success of students as evidence and data are collected at the end of the unit. Teachers reflect on student performance during and after the unit of study. Teachers take notes and *share* with colleagues what went well, what changes to make, and so on for the next unit of instruction.

Step One: Collaborative Teams Identify Learning Targets and Design Common Unit Tasks and Common Assessment Instruments

In a PLC culture, before the first lesson of the next unit of mathematics instruction begins, your collaborative teams (grade-level teams if elementary school and course-based teams if middle or high school) reach agreement on the design and proper use of high-quality, rigorous common assessment tasks (for formative in-class feedback) and assessment instruments (unit quizzes and tests) for all students during the unit.

However, to do so, the team must first reach clarity on and understanding of the expected learning targets for the unit as they answer the first of three critical questions for step one: (1) What are the identified learning standards? (2) What are the identified daily formative mathematical tasks? (3) What are the identified common assessment instruments? Your leadership role is to support and to pressure collaborative team step-one action as a reality of unit-by-unit practice for the team.

What Are the Identified Learning Standards?

What are the mathematical *procedural fluency* targets for proficiency in this unit of content? What are the mathematical *understanding* targets for proficiency? What are the Mathematical Practices that will be evident within the content's clusters *and* domains (and high school *conceptual categories*)? One of the advantages of the CCSS for mathematics is the well-identified learning target expectations in each domain, conceptual category, and cluster. Asking a student to understand something means teachers must formatively assess whether the student has understood it. Thus, a collective team discussion on what is intended by the learning targets for the unit, as well as the progression of the learning targets in the unit and to other units, will help the team better meet the vision of teaching to the CCSS *understanding* aspect of the standards.

Since the Common Core mathematics curriculum reduces the total number of learning targets, you should expect a greater depth and less breadth of topics per unit of study. There is, however, a greater expectation for the assessment of student *understanding* —the conceptual knowledge necessary for developing procedural fluency. As each collaborative team plans the unit calendar and pacing for the learning targets, adequate time should be built in to allow for formative in-class assessment feedback, corresponding instructional adjustments, and the use of appropriate tools and models for student demonstration of understanding. Once the teams understand the expected learning targets for the unit, they are ready for the next aspect of step one—identifying the

Common Core tasks that will be used to develop student understanding of the learning targets for the unit.

What Are the Identified Daily Formative Mathematical Tasks?

During step one, members of the collaborative team discuss the cognitive demand of the mathematics tasks that will be part of the daily lesson designs and used in class as part of the formative feedback process to students. Teachers' lesson-design planning involves the procedural skill *and* understanding level of the mathematical tasks and problems presented to the students during the unit of mathematical study.

The *Technical Issues in Large-Scale Assessment* (TILSA) project (Wise & Alt, 2005) provides insight into the design and implementation of teacher team–developed local assessment tasks. Adapted to fit the needs of your teacher team assessment and lesson-design work, figure 4.3 offers a resource to guide your collaborative team discussions and evaluate your collaborative teams' readiness to teach, assess, and learn *before* the new unit begins.

---

1. **Student opportunity to learn:** Do all students of the course or grade level have access to the same content? By the end of the unit will every teacher have covered the same content at the same level of rigor?

2. **Depth of knowledge:** Are cognitive requirements between the formative assessment tasks and the learning targets in the unit consistent for each teacher on the team? Is the same complexity of student knowledge (and skill) sought and required by all teachers for the mathematics unit through the tasks that students experience?

3. **Range of knowledge:** Is the range of content covered under each of the content standard clusters for the unit of knowledge similar from teacher to teacher in the grade level or course? Do all teachers of the course or grade level include daily common mathematical tasks that prepare students for procedural fluency as well as the conceptual understanding tasks that will be part of the common assessment instruments that all teachers use during the unit or chapter?

4. **Balance of representation:** Are learning targets for a particular cluster of standards given the same emphasis on the common assessment instruments all teachers on the collaborative team use?

5. **Source of challenge:** Does student assessment (test) performance actually depend on mastering the learning targets and not on irrelevant knowledge or skills?

Figure 4.3: Aligning learning targets with assessment instruments and tasks.

Visit **go.solution-tree.com/commoncore** for a reproducible version of this figure.

Your collaborative teams' preparation for the understanding aspects of the content standards is served through the lesson-design expectations of the CCSS Mathematical Practices as described in chapter 2. Common unit mathematical tasks need to be constructed so that Mathematical Practices (such as 3 and 5, pages 37–39 and 41–43, respectively) are part of the lesson design. The CCSS state it like this:

> One hallmark of mathematical understanding is the ability to justify, in a way appropriate to the student's mathematical maturity, *why* a particular

mathematical statement is true or where a mathematical rule comes from. Mathematical understanding and procedural skill are equally important, and both are assessable using mathematical tasks of sufficient richness. (NGA & CCSSO, 2010, p. 4)

As your team debates the use of assessment tasks that measure student understanding, step one is the critical first place where inequities in student mathematics learning are potentially manufactured. If you allow some members of the collaborative teams you lead to fail to reach agreement on the use and implementation of rich mathematical tasks during the lessons and assessments in each unit, then the learning outcomes for students will vary according to the individual teacher's task selection, and as a result the implementation gap only widens. The same will be true if your collaborative teams cannot reach agreement on the nature of viable student responses to such questions and the advancing and assessing questions that help to scaffold the learning target expectations for your students. Part of your leadership responsibility is to monitor the fair implementation of daily mathematical tasks that teach and assess for student understanding and to erase this inequity for students.

Equity in mathematics education requires your collaborative teams to design instructional lessons with rich mathematical tasks that engage students in observable mathematical informal discussions and serve as ongoing formative assessments with feedback (Kanold et al., 2012). Once the team understands the expected learning targets for the unit and has identified the Common Core tasks to develop in-class student understanding, then team members can discuss and develop common assessment instruments.

What Are the Identified Common Assessment Instruments?

When your collaborative teams create and design common assessment instruments together, they enhance the coherence and fidelity to student learning expectations across the school for all teachers. Furthermore, they provide the hope of greater readiness and continuity for the mathematics the students will take the following year. The wide variance in student task performance expectations (an inequity creator) from teacher to teacher is minimized when teachers work collaboratively to design assessments and tasks appropriate to the identified learning targets for the unit. As a school leader, you will want to carefully monitor all assessment instruments teachers give students. Thus, based on the identified learning targets for the unit or chapter of study, in your leadership capacity you must monitor the quality of the common assessment instruments—tests, quizzes, or projects—the team will use during the unit.

How do you decide if the unit-by-unit assessment instruments your teacher teams use are high quality? Figure 4.4 (page 94) provides an evaluation tool your collaborative teams can use to evaluate the quality of current tests and quizzes, as well as to create new grade-level or course assessment instruments.

The goal of using the evaluation tool in figure 4.4 is to help your teams diagnose whether or not the common assessment instruments would score 4s in all seven categories. Your collaborative teams could also create their own evaluation tool, using figures 4.3 and 4.4 as guides. The important point is that you as a school leader have

Assessment indicators	Description of Level 1	Requirements of the Indicator Are Not Present	Limited Requirements of This Indicator Are Present	Substantially Meets the Requirements of the Indicator	Fully Achieves the Requirements of the Indicator	Description of Level 4
Identification and emphasis on learning targets	Learning targets are unclear or absent from the assessment instrument. Too much attention is given to one target.	1	2	3	4	Clearly stated learning targets are on the assessment and connected to the assessment questions.
Visual presentation	Assessment is sloppy, disorganized, and difficult to read. There is no room for teacher feedback.	1	2	3	4	Assessment is neat, organized, easy to read, and well spaced. There is room for teacher feedback.
Time allotment	Few students can complete the assessment in the time allowed.	1	2	3	4	Test can be successfully completed in time allowed.
Clarity of directions	Directions are missing or unclear.	1	2	3	4	Directions are appropriate and clear.
Clear and appropriate scoring rubrics	Scoring rubric is either not in evidence or not appropriate for the assessment task.	1	2	3	4	Scoring rubric is clearly stated and appropriate for each problem.
Variety of assessment task formats	Assessment contains only one type of questioning strategy and no multiple choice. Calculator usage is not clear.	1	2	3	4	Test includes a variety of question types, assesses different formats, and includes calculator usage.
Question phrasing (precision)	Wording is vague or misleading. Vocabulary and precision of language is problematic for student understanding.	1	2	3	4	Vocabulary is direct, fair, and clearly understood. Students are expected to attend to precision in responses.
Balance of procedural fluency and demonstration of understanding	Test is not balanced for rigor. Emphasis is on procedural knowledge. Minimal cognitive demand for demonstration of understanding is present.	1	2	3	4	Test is balanced with product- and process-level questions. Higher-cognitive-demand and understanding tasks are present.

Figure 4.4: Evaluation tool for assessment instrument quality.

Visit **go.solution-tree.com/commoncore** for a reproducible version of this figure.

a crystal-clear basis for what you expect from high-quality assessment instruments given to students. Do current unit-by-unit assessments meet your standards of high quality? How do you know?

Thus, the value of any collaborative team-driven assessment depends on the extent to which the assessment instrument reflects the learning targets, can be used for a student formative learning process in the aftermath of the assessment, provides valid evidence of student learning, and results in a positive impact on student motivation and learning. It is your leadership responsibility to ensure the collaborative teams implement this vision for assessment.

Once your teams have completed these three critical lesson-planning tasks for step one, they are ready to teach the unit of instruction over the next twelve to sixteen days (recall the unit calendars in figures 3.1 and 3.2, pages 70 and 71, respectively), and step two of the teaching-assessing-learning cycle begins. Teachers use formative assessment strategies in class to advance and assess observable and formative student discussions and experiences around the unit learning targets.

Step Two: Teachers Implement Formative Assessment Classroom Strategies

Step two of the teaching-assessing-learning cycle occurs as part of the daily in-class formative assessment actions of the teacher team during the unit of study. Team members intentionally plan for and implement both formal and informal learning structures and tasks as outlined in chapters 2 and 3 that will provide ongoing student engagement and descriptive feedback around the elements of the learning targets as well as the CCSS Mathematical Practices.

This step highlights the work of the collaborative teams to present the daily common mathematical tasks (designed in step one) in an engaging and formative learning environment and then to use appropriate formative assessment feedback strategies to determine student understanding of the intended learning targets.

According to Wiliam (2011):

> When formative assessment practices are integrated into the minute-to-minute and day-by-day classroom activities of teachers, substantial increases in student achievement—of the order of a 70 to 80% increase in the speed of learning are possible. . . . Moreover, these changes are not expensive to produce. . . . The currently available evidence suggests that there is nothing else remotely affordable that is likely to have such a large effect. (p. 161)

You should not allow your collaborative teams to ignore this wise advice.

Popham (2008), Ginsburg and Dolan (2011), and Wiliam (2011) have suggested several "informal" strategies of assessment *for* learning and checks for understanding that can provide teachers valuable insight into the level of student understanding as a lesson unfolds. An additional advantage of these formative assessment strategies is that they increase the level of student engagement, a key characteristic of classroom environments that promote high student achievement (Wiliam, 2011). Some of these strategies are provided to teachers in the grade-level books for the series and are available online for your reference in this book. Your teacher teams can use these strategies as boundary markers for team discussion and in-class observation and support as teams implement the Mathematical Practices (student practices) in their lesson designs. Consider the following:

- Effective questioning during whole-class discussions
- Mini or large whiteboard responses for small-group discourse
- Traffic lights or red and green disks for student response
- All-student response systems such as SMART boards
- Diagnostic interview questions with small-group student teams

As your collaborative teams seek to design mathematics tasks, teachers should consider the following *formative assessment feedback* questions.

1. How do we expect students will express their ideas, questions, insights, and difficulties?

2. Where and when will and should the most significant conversations be taking place (student to teacher, student to student, teacher to student)?

3. How approachable and encouraging should we be as students explore? Do students use and value each other as reliable and valuable learning resources?

When school leaders help teacher teams reach agreement on the types of formative questions to be used in class, it results in improved in-class teacher adjustments to instruction. Daily demonstrations of student learning will be based on a more coherent *team-based* practice. However, this will not be sufficient. If during the best teacher-designed moments of classroom formative assessment students fail to *take action* on evidence of continued areas of difficulty, then the teaching-assessing-learning cycle is stopped for the student. This will be an important focus of future class observations. You will need to determine whether students respond to the formative feedback the teacher provides.

Step Three: Students Take Action on In-Class Formative Assessment Feedback

Effective formative assessment is not only about teachers using evidence to modify and adjust instruction but also about students using the data to make their own adjustments in the processes they use to achieve the learning targets (Popham, 2008; Wiliam, 2011). Do students learn to take more responsibility for their learning by using the feedback teachers provide them? This is the goal of step three in the assessment cycle.

Rick Stiggins and colleagues (2006), in *Classroom Assessment for Student Learning: Doing It Right—Using It Well*, state, "Few interventions have the same level of impact as assessment *for* learning. The most intriguing result is that while all students show achievement gains, the largest gains accrue to the lowest achievers" (p. 37). Thus, you should challenge your teams to think and plan beyond the sole use of in-class daily checks for understanding as an accountability measure for keeping students on task to thinking of assessment as way to provide formative learning action for students.

Stiggins et al. (2006) suggest strategies teachers can use to support students in taking more responsibility for their own learning. Several of these strategies are adapted in figure 4.5. They provide insight into the nature of teacher-designed but *student-led* formative assessment *actions*.

Strategy One: Provide a Clear and Understandable Vision of the Learning Target

Teachers share with students the CCSS cluster, learning targets, and prior-knowledge understanding expectations in advance of teaching the lesson or unit, giving the assignment, or doing the activity. They provide students with scoring guides written in plain language so they can understand them. More importantly, the teachers develop and design scoring criteria and rubrics with students.

Strategy Two: Use Examples and Models of Strong and Weak Work

Teachers use models of strong and weak work, such as anonymous student work, work from life beyond school, and their own work. They begin with work that demonstrates strengths and weaknesses related to problems students will commonly experience, especially the problems or tasks that require student demonstrations of understanding. They ask students to discuss with peers strengths and weaknesses of given solutions or strategies used to obtain a solution to problems posed in class or on a common assessment instrument. They also ask students to select examples of their strong and weak work and explain the reason for the selection.

Strategy Three: Offer Regular Descriptive Feedback

During and after the unit, teachers offer descriptive feedback instead of grades on practice work. Descriptive feedback should reflect students' strengths and weaknesses with respect to the specific learning targets they are trying to achieve in a given assignment. Feedback is most effective when it is timely and identifies what students are doing right as well as what they need to work on next and then requires students to act on that feedback.

Strategy Four: Teach Students to Self-Assess and Set Goals

Self-assessment is a necessary part of learning, not an add-on that teachers do if they have the time or the "right" type of students. Self-assessment includes asking students do the following:

- Identify their strengths and areas for improvement for specific learning targets throughout the unit

- Offer descriptive feedback to classmates

- Use teacher feedback, feedback from other students, or their own self-assessment to identify what they need to work on and set goals for future learning and then take action on those goals

---

Figure 4.5: Formative assessment strategies for student engagement and action.

Visit **go.solution-tree.com/commoncore** for a reproducible version of this figure.

Help your various collaborative teams plan mathematics lessons throughout the unit of study that will ensure students know about their in-class progress. All teachers on the team must require student-led action steps for responding to the formative feedback that students are receiving from the teacher as well as from *other students*. As Wiliam (2011) mentions, "Providing effective feedback is very difficult. Get it wrong and the students give up, reject the feedback or choose an easier goal" (p. 119). A key to Wiliam's finding is that feedback functions formatively "only if the information fed back to the learner is used by the learner for improving his or her performance" (p. 120). This gives new meaning and understanding to the teacher's responsibility for helping students get "unstuck" in class (without watering down the cognitive demand of the task) while simultaneously helping students to think differently about a problem or its extension as the lesson unfolds. This is essentially the basis for the *assessing* and *advancing* questions in figure 2.12 (page 53).The strategies in figure 4.5 (page 97) are designed to place much of the in-class feedback response and action onto student ownership.

As described in strategy four, self-assessment is a necessary part of learning. Students need to identify their own strengths and areas for improvement (with more teacher guidance and direction at the elementary than the secondary level) and use teacher feedback, feedback from other students, or their own self-assessment to identify what they need to work on as they set goals for future learning. Assessment then comes to be viewed by the students as something you *do* in order to focus your energy and effort for future work and study. Your role as a school leader is once again not so much to know exactly how to do this (you can allow the teacher team some freedom to decide) but to ensure that the team honors the vision of student action on feedback in step three.

As Wiliam (2007b) indicates, in order to "improve the quality of learning within the system, to be formative, feedback needs to contain an implicit or explicit recipe for future action" (p. 1062). This requires teachers to think about how daily and weekly feedback from peers or from you can be used for student-initiated action and engagement with the feedback.

Thus, students and teachers share the responsibility for successful implementation of the in-class formative assessment practices. Students who can demonstrate *understanding* connect to the learning targets for a unit and can reflect on their individual progress toward that target. Students can establish learning goals and actions they will take in order to reach the targets, and teachers support students' progress by using immediate and effective feedback not only during the daily classroom conversations but also as part of the common assessment instrument feedback process used in step four.

Step Four: Students Use Assessment Instruments From Step One for Motivation, Reflection, and Action

The first three steps in the teaching-assessing-learning cycle may already be part of the assessment paradigm in your school or district. Your collaborative teams do write common assessment instruments together, they do design effective formative assessment classroom tasks, and they do use strategies that ensure their students take action on the feedback they provide on their in-class daily classroom performance. However, it is very rare to find school mathematics teachers or collaborative teams that use common assessment instruments such as quizzes and tests as part of a formative process of learning. It is in step four that the old paradigm of testing primarily for grading purposes (an end goal) becomes secondary as the new paradigm of using assessment instruments and tools for formative assessment purposes (a means goal) emerges.

Wiliam (2007b) makes the distinction between using *assessment* instruments for the purposes of (1) monitoring, (2) diagnosing, or (3) formatively assessing. He states:

> An assessment *monitors* learning to the extent it provides information about whether the student, class, school or system is learning or not; it is *diagnostic* to the extent it provides information about what is going wrong, and it is *formative* to the extent it provides information about what to do about it. (p. 1062)

In school mathematics, the process may look like this. An eighth-grade student studies for and is given an assessment instrument (call it a test, quiz, or quest; the name is not relevant to the purpose) midway through a unit on the CCSS content standards N-RN.1 and 2. The collaborative team designs the midway assessment instrument tool (quiz) and the scoring rubrics for the tool and decides the assessment tool has a scoring value of 60 points. The student scores 35 out of 60 correct for a score of 58.3 percent. The class score or average is 72 percent. This is the *monitoring* or *grading* assessment function. This function allows the teacher to assign student grades. Furthermore, of the three purposes—monitoring, diagnosing, and formatively assessing—it is the *least useful* for improving and motivating student thinking and achievement toward the learning targets.

As Wiliam (2011) describes:

> [Effective feedback] should cause thinking. It should be focused; it should be related to the learning goals that have been shared with students; and it should be more work for the recipient than the donor. Indeed, the whole purpose of feedback should be to increase the extent to which students are owners of their own learning. (p. 132)

At the heart of teacher feedback to students on such a midunit quiz should be some metrics that would allow the assessment instrument to be used beyond the monitoring purpose of assigning a grade. This will require you to help teachers understand how to help students take the time necessary to use the feedback they receive on the assessment instrument to improve their work (Wiliam, 2011). One way for teachers to do this is to include exam instrument elements that allow for diagnostic and then formative student action.

In the case of the 58 percent student response, a self-analysis of a specific student's performance might indicate that he or she was not demonstrating success on the learning target. A score of 58.3 percent means nothing unless the student is able to track the exact learning targets that were strengths and weaknesses on the assessment tool. Thus, a *diagnostic* assessment is rarely sufficient for the student. Diagnostic assessments do not tell students what they need to do differently (other than try harder). However, when the student uses specific teacher *or* peer feedback, the assessment result has the potential to be *formative* for the student and improve performance on the learning targets necessary to master the standards.

One way to do this is to include exam instrument elements that allow for a diagnostic and formative student action. A collaborative team tool can be used by teachers to help students learn from their assessment and quiz mistakes. You can view a sample tool in the online resources for this book and should take note of several important elements. The student diagnostic tool asks each student to examine his or her areas of strengths and weakness on the quiz or test instrument.

The students focus on specific learning targets that were strengths as well as those that were weaknesses. Students are then required to "take action" by creating a plan for improvement in that learning target before the next assessment performance is required. The specific plan might include: "To prepare for the chapter 1 test I will redo my notes, which cover my areas of weakness; retry book examples, which cover my areas of weakness; seek help at the learning center; meet with my teacher; and know the vocabulary."

Wiliam (2011) cites Randy Bennett (2009) when he states, "It is an oversimplification to say that formative assessment is *only* a matter of process or *only* a matter of instrumentation. Good processes require good instruments and good instruments are useless unless they are used intelligently" (p. 40). Your teacher teams will be wise to spend significant time designing common unit assessment instruments that can be used *intelligently*—ensuring all students in a course or grade level benefit from both good tests (instruments) and good formative processes for student use and action on the assessment instrument results and feedback. (Visit **go.solution-tree.com/commoncore** for additional samples of student self-assessment feedback and response form samples from the grade-level books in the series.)

However, the assessment cycle is not complete until teacher teams work together during the unit of instruction and at the end of the unit of instruction to discuss and decide how to respond to the student assessment evidence collected during the unit.

Step Five: Collaborative Teams Use Ongoing Student Assessment Feedback to Improve Instruction

In step five, your collaborative teams take the time (you may need to help them learn how to do this) to use students' assessment results to change instruction for the next instructional cluster or unit. This allows the test or quiz assessment instruments to become *formative* for the teachers. Success in step five depends on success in step one—writing and designing common summative assessment instruments in advance of teaching the next unit of instruction. The collaborative team's assessment has its greatest payoff in this final collaborative step, using the student performance results to make future instructional decisions together.

It will also allow collaborative teams, in hindsight, to evaluate the quality of the assessment questions; indicate improvements for next year; and discuss the quality of the descriptive student feedback, the accuracy of the predetermined student scoring rubrics, and the fidelity of students' grades for the unit. Collaborative teams can also use the results to identify potential learning targets and assessment questions that may need to be repeated as part of the next unit of study.

In the teaching-assessing-learning cycle (figure 4.2, page 90), assessment is in the middle of the cycle—it is not at the *end*. This placement is a fundamental shift for school mathematics teachers. Student learning becomes a *result* of in-class daily formative assessment as well as the assessment instruments such as tests and quizzes the teams use—not the other way around. Collaborative teams take future actions that improve teaching and instruction based on the latest assessment evidence.

You can use figure 4.6 to help your collaborative teams reflect on their performance during and at the end of the unit. Figure 4.6 also highlights questions to guide the teacher lesson-planning and lesson-revision processes. As a team, teachers should reflect on their performance during and at the end of the unit to improve instruction for the next unit of learning.

---

1. How much of the unit's content was taught through student exploration or student questioning (instead of teacher-centered lecture)?

   What evidence is there of a climate of mutual respect as students participate in mathematical discussions and provide meaningful feedback and critique the reasoning of other students?

   How well did students make and test predictions, conjectures, hypotheses, and estimations with the teacher and with one another? (Mathematical Practices 2, 3, 5, and 6)

2. What kinds of in-class formative assessments did the teacher use to design the lesson as well as evaluate the effectiveness of the lesson?

   How well did the teacher provide descriptive feedback to the students, engage students in the lesson, and develop student interest through lesson design creativity?

   How well were fundamental learning targets taught with evidence of student understanding?

   How well did students reflect on their own learning as it relates to the learning cluster and learning targets for this unit?

3. What CCSS Mathematical Practices did the teacher and students use to learn the mathematics content standards?

   What evidence is there that students were part of a learning community?

   How did students communicate their ideas to one another and the teacher?

   How did the teacher's questions elicit student thinking and other students' respectful critiquing of that reasoning? (Mathematical Practice 3)

4. What kinds of questions and conjectures did students propose in the early stages of the unit lessons, and what kinds of student-led summative exercises were used to measure student understanding and learning for the unit cluster?

Source: Adapted from Kanold et al., 2012.

Figure 4.6: Critical lesson-planning and reflection questions.

Visit **go.solution-tree.com/commoncore** for a reproducible version of this figure.

By using the unit lesson-design questions (a formative assessment process for your teams) in figure 4.6 (page 101) as part of the teacher team reflection and feedback, your teams will have a greater chance of gathering data during and after the unit that will inform aspects of the next unit of instruction throughout the year as well as inform practice for a similar unit next year. This allows you to keep assessment right where it belongs—in the middle of instruction and as a means and not an ends to improvement. Working with your collaborative teams, you may help support and encourage them to redesign lessons several times during future units of study, based on the formative feedback collected during these team discussions.

The five-step assessment cycle has a powerful impact on student achievement and learning. More than just becoming masters of content delivery, teachers also become masters at using varied assessment tasks and tools, including the formative classroom assessment strategies (listed in step three) that help students take greater ownership of their learning.

As the mathematics unit comes to an end, students who have received formative feedback (allowing them to correct errors *before and after* the final unit assessment on the cluster of learning targets) perform at significantly improved rates of learning (Wiliam, 2007b). After a unit's instruction is over, the teacher and the student must reflect on the results of their work and be willing to use the unit assessment instruments to serve a formative feedback purpose. For teachers, this means a commitment to understanding one of their most powerful assessment weapons—using grades as a form of feedback to motivate student learning and effort.

Summative Moments in the Formative Feedback Paradigm

For many students, traditional mathematics teacher grading practices destroy motivation and learning. As Alfie Kohn (2011) dryly indicates:

> You know it's ironic: A lot of us [students] are less interested in learning— and therefore won't do as well—precisely because you've made it all about grades. Hey, I guess you can say you've earned our lack of motivation. (p. 28)

Furthermore, as Wiliam (2011) notes, "As soon as students get a grade the learning stops" (p. 123). *The student learning stops.* Think about a student in your school that receives a summative grade of 58.6 percent on a quiz or test instrument. Did assigning him or her that grade cause (motivate) the student to learn the 41.4 percent of the test that was not correct or proficient? This is the old paradigm: the unit or chapter is over— in some cases, more than a week ago or more—by the time the tests are returned. There is no future action. The next unit has begun anyway.

However, there is hope. In a PLC, collaborative teams can overcome the great demotivator that results in using common assessment tools only for the purpose of assigning grades. The hope lies squarely in the team's ability to shift to a new assessment paradigm about grading—grades should serve primarily as a form of effective formative feedback to students and to enhance the teaching-assessing-learning cycle.

Reeves (2011a) establishes this primary purpose of grading as a form of student feedback to improve their performance. Reeves (2011a) cites Thomas R. Guskey (2000): "In fact, when students are rewarded only with feedback on their [assessment instrument] performance and are not subjected to a grade, their performance is better than when they are graded" (p. 105). Perhaps the challenge for your collaborative teams is to determine how long into a school semester teachers could go without assigning any grades to students. Imagine teachers only using homework, quizzes, and tests as formative tools for student ownership and action on weak learning targets in need of continued attention and learning progress action. Yet, the school world you live in demands grades or at least mastery reports. However, in a PLC, your teams can structure those grades within certain boundaries that support the use of the assessment tools that teachers grade and students use as formative tools for learning as described in step four of the cycle.

Thus, your collaborative teams must discuss whether their *collective* grading practices act as feedback to students in such a way that motivates continued and improved effort and performance. Can your teams develop students' mathematical *habits of mind* in which every assessment opportunity is viewed as a formative learning moment?

Think about the current grading practices your collaborative teams use. How do you know whether they're effective? Reeves (2011a) provides four boundary markers as a basis to frame and measure your teams' current grading practices. In a PLC culture, grading is viewed as a form of effective feedback to students, based on the following four characteristics.

1. **Grades must be accurate:** Do grades on tests, quizzes, and projects reflect actual student knowledge and performance on the expected learning targets?

2. **Grades must be specific:** Do grades provide sufficiently specific information to help parents and students identify areas for improvement (formative, not just diagnostic) with student action long before the final summative grade is assigned?

3. **Grades must be timely:** Do grades on tests, quizzes, and projects provide a steady stream of immediate and corrective teacher feedback to students?

4. **Grades must be fair:** Do grades on tests, quizzes, and projects reflect solely on the student's work, not other characteristics of the student? Are grades based on some form of student comparison such as assigning grades on a curve—based on other students' performance in the class?

These boundaries on your teams' assessment practices act as part of an effective feedback process and address deeply held time-honored paradigms about grading. It is your responsibility to monitor and then evaluate the quality of current grading practices in your sphere of influence and determine if they reside within these four essential boundaries. Most importantly, whatever assessment instrument is used for determining a student's grade, it must also provide an opportunity for the student to improve his or her grade.

Grading Feedback Must Be Accurate

Grading practices on any graded assessment have the potential to create a major inequity. Consequently, you must ensure that your collaborative teams have made this issue an intentional focus. When assessments are graded in isolation, fidelity to the grading process and indicators for what a grade means are nonexistent.

The intent of accurate feedback on an exam is to give students *information* about their mathematical understanding of the learning targets for the assessment. As described in step one (figure 4.2, page 90), your collaborative teams can ensure greater accuracy in their grading feedback by looking at student work (protocols) together and collaboratively scoring the mathematical tasks on the assessment instruments. As you lead discussions of each task, learning targets associated with tasks, and the requirements of each task, you provide the guidance that enables the teachers to identify student successes and misconceptions. These rich conversations also shape the teams' shared content knowledge of the mathematical concepts as you articulate how students should be graded on various concepts and skills.

Your collaborative teams can improve the *accuracy* of their grading feedback on the team-designed common assessments by using team time to:

1. Establish agreed-on scoring rubrics for all assessment questions

2. Conduct group or team scoring (grading) practice sessions on a sample of student work and responses

3. Discuss and resolve differences of opinion regarding discrepant scores by multiple scoring of student samples by different teachers, checking for agreement on the student grade for papers (inter-rater reliability), and reaching agreement on the score for the student's grade (calibration of teacher grading)

Reeves (2011a) points out that collaborative scoring techniques not only improve accuracy of the initial grades students receive on the assessment but also save time for teachers. As teachers work collaboratively, they will, over time, realize improvements in speed for grading feedback and for accuracy in using the assessment scoring rubrics.

If this is not consistent from teacher to teacher on the team, again, another inequity is created for the student learning response.

Grading Feedback Must Be Specific

Scoring and grading a lab, project, quiz, or a test instrument has traditionally been a deeply personal and private act. In this new paradigm of using assessment tools such as projects, quizzes, and tests for formative purposes, the type of specific feedback teachers provide to students as they score the exams must be consistent.

What should *specific feedback* look like? Feedback that is limited to a total test's percent score along with a letter grade is too general and only serves a diagnostic purpose.

However, feedback that is process or task oriented and requires the student to respond to the errors (and the teacher's feedback about the errors) will increase student achievement over time. This is especially true in vertically connected (students need last year's content knowledge to understand this year's) courses such as mathematics. This is the value of step four in the assessment cycle.

With your help, collaborative teams can learn to design an agreed-on scoring rubric used for each question on the lab, project, quiz, or test assessment instrument. This rubric is a prime example of specific feedback. Deciding as a team how much each question should be worth and what type of errors will receive partial credit with specific feedback on the error creates consistent feedback across all teachers on the team. When students receive scoring rubrics for various assessment tasks before they complete their work, they have a better understanding of how they will be assessed. Using collaboratively designed scoring rubrics decreases the subjectivity of a grade and impacts overall grading accuracy for the course. (Visit www.insidemathematics.org or http://map.mathshell.org/materials/index.php for specific feedback with rubrics.)

Once students know that the grade is more than just a one-shot deal and that they can actually learn from the specific feedback the teacher provides to them on the assessment instrument or exam—both the scoring feedback and the written feedback to certain question errors—students are more motivated to learn. However, the positive impact of that feedback is lost *if* the teacher fails to allow students to rework their errors for an improved grade or fails to allow them to improve a weak learning target area (Canady & Hotchkiss, 1989).

Grading Feedback Must Be Timely

Timeliness—the third characteristic of effective feedback—often needs to be improved. Reeves (2011a) indicates that timeliness refers to feedback provided to students with sufficient promptness to influence their future performance. Does that describe the work of every teacher on your teams? Grading feedback that is accurate and specific has no benefit if it is provided to students too late to impact their future performance. How do you help your collaborative teams attend to this critical area of feedback?

The teacher's grading feedback needs to be *immediate.* In the old assessment paradigm, the timeliness of grading feedback was a discretionary task of each teacher. This is not so in the new paradigm. Your discussions about grading practices with the teams will remind them of what it means to be timely with grading feedback. You should make clear that an assessment should not be scheduled if the teacher or teacher team knows the feedback will not be provided to the students within one or two days. Students are more motivated to prepare for an assessment if they know they will receive feedback either the same or next day (Hattie, 2009). They know to take the assessment seriously because the teacher places high value on the assessment as well.

Grading Feedback Must Be Fair

How do you know if the teacher's grading practices are fair for every student in the course? First, fair evaluation of a student must be based primarily on academic performance. Wormeli (2006) states, "Differentiation is doing what is fair for students" (p. 3). By using differentiation strategies to prepare students for the quiz and test assessments, teachers are not making the content easier; they are making the content accessible. Discussions with your collaborative teams can focus on the factors that detract from fairness in grading feedback. For example, it would be disingenuous for teachers to lower their expectations for standards proficiency because of the gender, ethnicity, or socioeconomic status of students.

As indicated under timely feedback, you need to ensure that the teachers are also willing to allow student demonstration of performance *over time* before the summative grade is assigned. To ensure equitable grading of students' understanding and skill level, teachers need to allow multiple attempts of mastery on the unit learning targets. This is one of the great benefits of the assessment cycle. Wormeli (2006) notes, "It is more reasonable to allow students every opportunity to show their best side, not just one opportunity. . . . We are teaching adults in the making, not adults" (p. 31).

Finally, as a school leader, you must ask your collaborative teams, "Are you using fair components to determine semester grades? How do missing assignments affect a student's overall grade? Are students allowed to turn in homework late, or do they receive a zero? If students are allowed multiple attempts at mastering the learning targets, how do you address the grading of retake assessment instruments? Is the process fair and motivating for all students?" These questions help team members examine their overall grading practices and make necessary changes to ensure fairness. Visit www.allthingsplc .info for help in how to negotiate the difficult team conversations that are part of reaching these agreements.

Effective Summative Grading Practices

To clearly establish a relationship between a student's grade and his or her demonstration of mathematical understanding, your collaborative teams should engage in honest conversations about their beliefs related to grading (this includes the use of a standards- or mastery-based report card). Figure 4.7 provides an activity to use with your teams as you help them investigate potential areas for grading inequity and bias. You can use this activity to search for your own biases as a leader and to better understand whether or not the teams you lead and influence use practices that motivate or destroy student effort and learning.

By answering the questions in figure 4.7, you and your teams will discover a lot about your built-in biases and issues related to the accuracy, timeliness, specificity, and fairness of grades.

In your collaborative team, complete the following, and describe your practices during a grading period.

1. List all components used to determine a student's grade in your course, such as tests, quizzes, homework, projects, and so on. Are the components and the percentages assigned to each component the same for every teacher on your team? Do the percentages align with the actual percentage of total points?

2. What is the grading scale your team uses? Is it the same for every member? How does your team address the issue of the "really bad" F, such as a 39 percent that distorts a student's overall grade performance?

3. What position does your team follow for assigning zeros to students? If teachers assign zeros, how does your team address the elimination of those zeros before the summative grade is assigned? (The goal is not to assign students a zero—in a PLC, the goal is to motivate every student to do his or her mathematics homework, prepare for tests, complete assignments, and so on). Do you:

   ○ Drop one homework grade from the grading period?

   ○ Drop one quiz or test score per grading period?

   ○ Allow for student makeup or retesting on weak learning targets?

4. What is your collaborative team's position on makeup work for class? Is your makeup policy fair for students, and do all members apply it equitably? Does your makeup policy encourage and motivate all students to keep trying?

5. How does your collaborative team prepare students for a major unit exam or quiz? Do all team members provide students with the same formative opportunities for preparing for the learning targets?

6. How does your team provide for the immediate and corrective feedback on major quiz and test instruments? Do all students receive results, identify areas of weakness, and then act on those results within two to three days?

7. Does your collaborative team average letter grades or use total points throughout the grading period? Explain your current grading system. How does your team address the inequity caused by total points as part of a summative grade (in which it is impossible to offset zeros and one really bad F with enough good grades to accurately represent overall performance)?

8. How does your team provide for the strategic use of technology tools as an aspect of evaluating student performance during the unit?

Source: Adapted from Kanold, 2011b.

Figure 4.7: A collaborative team analysis of grading practices.

Visit **go.solution-tree.com/commoncore** for a reproducible version of this figure.

Looking Ahead

Implementing Common Core mathematics is not likely to alter the scrutiny and pressure you will face as a school leader regarding these large-scale assessments. Under the curriculum guidelines of the CCSS, a state assessment system must now provide a coherent and consistent formative system anchored in college- and career-ready expectations. Two state consortia are designing state-level common assessments for the standards. These common state assessments will reflect the expectations for the CCSS content with large-scale assessments that measure beyond the traditional multiple-choice, bubble-in answer sheets. As Achieve (2010) notes, it is the hope and the expectation that these new exams will:

> Improve the quality and types of items included in on-demand tests to create more cognitively-challenging tasks that measure higher-order thinking and analytic skills, such as reasoning and problem solving; move beyond a single, end-of-year test to open the door for performance measures and extended tasks that do a better job of measuring important college- and career-ready skills and model exemplary forms of classroom instruction. (p. 1)

As mentioned in chapter 1, two consortia representing the majority of states are developing assessments aligned with the CCSS: the SMARTER Balanced Assessment Consortium (SBAC) and the Partnership for Assessment of Readiness for College and Careers (PARCC). Both PARCC and SBAC intend to provide myriad online tests that will include a mix of constructed-response items, performance-based tasks, and computer-enhanced items that require the application of knowledge and skills. Both assessment consortia are intending to provide summative and interim assessment options within the assessment system. You should check your state website for the latest information about progress of the assessment consortia, or visit www.parcconline.org/about-parcc or www.smarterbalanced.org for more information.

Regardless of the opportunity for the PARCC and SBAC assessments to provide school districts formative assessment information on the state assessment instruments, what will make the most difference in terms of student learning is the shorter cycle, unit-by-unit classroom-based formative assessments described in this chapter. As Wiliam (2007a) writes, "If students have left the classroom before teachers have made adjustments to their teaching on the basis of what they have learned about students' achievement, then they are already playing catch-up" (p. 191).

As Tate and Rousseau (2007) indicate in *Engineering Changes in Mathematics Education*, "Students' opportunities to learn mathematics are influenced by the assessment policies of the local district. Assessment policies often influence the nature of pedagogy in the classroom" (p. 1222). The questions every school leader must ask are, "What is the vision of our assessment policies and practices in this department?" "How will we work together so that assessment can become a motivational student bridge in the assessment cycle in our school?" As you develop your response around a vision of assessment as a means and not an end, there will be major positive impact on student motivation and the level of improved student learning in your mathematics program.

Chapter 4 Extending My Understanding

1. Using the definition of formative assessment on page 89, describe how your current assessment practices either do or do not meet this standard.

2. High-quality assessment practices function to integrate *formative* assessment processes for adult and student learning by:

   a. Implementing formative assessment classroom strategies and advancing and assessing questions that check for student understanding during classroom instruction

   b. Using assessment instruments such as quizzes and tests as tools to support a formative learning process for teachers and students to take action

   How can your collaborative teams use common classroom assessment instruments, along with other formative assessment information sources collected each day, to advance student learning and support students' active involvement in taking ownership of their own learning?

3. Examine the assessment cycle (page 90). For the following five steps for each of your teams under your leadership and direction, rate your current level of implementation (0 percent to 100 percent), and explain what each team might do to improve this assessment practice during the school year. Note there are two different step-one responsibilities.

   ○ **Step one (in-class formative assessment):** How well do the teachers understand and develop *in advance of teaching* the unit of study, the student learning targets, content standard clusters, and domains; the common student assessment tasks that will align with those targets; the use of technology to develop understanding of those targets; and the homework that will be assigned?

   ○ **Step one (test instrument formative assessment):** How well do the teachers identify the agreed-on common assessment instruments, scoring rubrics for those instruments, and grading procedures that will *accurately reflect student achievement* of the learning targets for the unit?

   ○ **Step two:** How well do the teachers use daily classroom assessments that are formative, build student confidence, and require student goal setting and reflection on the learning targets they know and don't know?

   ○ **Step three:** How well do the teachers use diagnostic and formative assessment feedback that provides *frequent, descriptive, timely,* and *accurate* feedback for students during the unit—allowing members of the collaborative teams as well as their students to take action on specific insights regarding their strengths as well as how to improve?

   ○ **Step four:** How well do the teachers, as members of collaborative teams, ask students to *adjust and take action* based on the results of the common assessment instruments (quizzes and tests) used during the unit of study? Do they allow that action to improve student grades?

○ **Step five:** How well do the teachers, as members of collaborative teams, *adjust and differentiate instruction* based on the results of formative assessment evidence as well as the common assessment instruments used during the unit of study?

4. Work with your collaborative teams to examine figure 4.7 (page 107). Discuss your current grading practices, and judge whether or not you believe current practices in your school meet the standards for effective feedback and result in motivating student performance. Discuss how your teams' grading practices could improve.

Online Resources

Visit **go.solution-tree.com/commoncore** for links to these online resources.

- **Mathematics Common Core Coalition (www.nctm.org/standards/math commoncore):** The site includes materials and links to information and resources that the organizations of the coalition provide to the public and the education community about the CCSS for mathematics.

- **Mathematics Assessment Project (http://map.mathshell.org.uk/materials):** The Mathematics Assessment Program (MAP) brings life to the Common Core State Standards in a way that will help teachers and their students turn their aspirations for achieving them into classroom realities. MAP contains exemplar formative lessons, assessment instruments, and rich mathematical tasks.

- **Partnership for Assessment of Readiness for College and Careers (www .parcconline.org):** This site provides content frameworks, sample instructional units, sample assessment tasks, professional development assessment modules, and more.

- **SMARTER Balanced Assessment Consortium (www.smarterbalanced.org):** This site provides mathematics draft content considerations and various assessment-related resources.

- **NCTM's assessment resources (www.nctm.org/resources/content.aspx ?id=12650):** Resources such as a framework for evaluating large-scale assessments, NCTM's position statement on high-stakes assessment, and various other publications are available through this webpage.

- **Numeric pattering (www.insidemathematics.org/index.php/classroom -video-visits/public-lessons-numerical-patterning):** This resource provides a re-engagement lesson for learners to revisit a problem-solving task.

CHAPTER 5

Leading the Implementation of Required Response to Intervention

Ultimately there are two kinds of schools: learning enriched schools and learning impoverished schools. I have yet to see a school where the learning curves … of the adults were steep upward and those of the students were not. Teachers and students go hand and hand as learners … or they don't go at all

—Roland Barth

As the curriculum is written, the unit learning targets are set, and the assessments are in place, teachers' current instructional processes need to meet the needs of *each* student in their courses. As you read the Common Core State Standards for mathematics for the first time, you might think about the students in each class, school site, or district and wonder, "Will they be able to respond positively to the expected complexity for each grade level? Can teachers develop the CCSS Mathematical Practices in each student? How will *each* student be able to succeed with rich and meaningful mathematical tasks? Are there different learning opportunities for different groups of students, depending on their mathematics ability or diversity? How can teachers generate equitable learning experiences so that each student is prepared to meet the demands of the Common Core mathematics as described in this book?" The key to answering these questions is the essential work of the collaborative teams you lead. To create an equitable mathematics program, teachers and school leaders alike must ensure current structures for teaching and learning will generate greater access, equity, and opportunity to learn for each student in each grade level or course.

No matter how hard teachers try, their current instructional practices can be improved so that students' opportunities to learn are fair and impartial. In its equity position paper, NCSM (2008a) describes research-informed practices that support the vision of equity. In mathematics education, as described throughout this book and this series, inequities are created when students do not have the same access and opportunities to learn based on the independent decisions of those serving on your collaborative teams.

NCTM (2000), in *Principles and Standards for School Mathematics*, defines *equity* in terms of having high expectations *and* support. NCTM (2008b) encourages the:

> Use of increasingly intensive and effective instructional interventions for students who struggle in mathematics. . . . When implementing appropriate

interventions for each mathematics learner, teachers must possess strong backgrounds in mathematical content knowledge for teaching, pedagogical content knowledge, and a wide range of instructional strategies. (p. 1)

Vision of Equity

The focus of this chapter is to define equity for mathematics teaching and learning and describe your leadership efforts and your collaborative teams' responses to students who are not meeting the expected standards. This chapter describes the fundamental paradigm shift for mathematics intervention and the collective response (from you and your collaborative teams, school, or district) necessary for student learning. In a PLC, collaborative teams ensure students have equitable learning environments that include the instruction, content, assessment, and grading procedures as described in chapters 2 through 4.

As part of the mathematics intervention paradigm shift in your PLC, your teams will be required, not just invited, to stay focused on how to monitor student access to meaningful mathematics. As you begin to monitor CCSS teaching and learning and pursue a vision for equity in your school or district, you can use the essential questions in table 5.1 as a guide to discuss equity in your collaborative teams.

Table 5.1: Essential Questions for Equity

Essential Questions	Comments
How are inequalities regarding student access to the best teaching and learning for the CCSS curriculum being addressed in your school or district? Are there certain subpopulations of students that do not have access to the college-preparatory curriculum? (This includes CCSS grade-level content in elementary school.)	
Are all students able to participate in college preparatory mathematics in your school or district? What do the data reveal about student success in mathematics as students get older?	
Are diverse student populations represented in your college- and career-readiness grade levels or courses (grade-level CCSS courses in grades K–8)?	
Are teachers implementing common and shared instructional tasks consistently?	
Is there coherence in implementation between teachers on horizontally and vertically developed mathematics concepts and progressions?	

Essential Questions	Comments
Does each student have access to the best instructional resources and tools available to the teachers?	
How are assessment instruments used to drive teacher teams' instructional decisions?	
How do teachers and their collaborative teams respond to students who have traditionally been underperformers?	
Do the teacher teams identify interventions and supports for students who are not meeting the expected standards and provide those supports immediately?	

Visit **go.solution-tree.com/commoncore** for a reproducible version of this table.

To pursue equity, you, your teams, and other mathematics leaders need to break through the social issues and disparities to engage each student in rich mathematics experiences. Effective collaborative teams actively pursue current barriers to student success and find ways to overcome them. It is no longer acceptable to say, "Our kids can't" in collaborative meetings. Through collaboration, you and the teams you lead work toward a common vision holding shared values and beliefs about student learning, ultimately leading toward a school culture that will support academic achievement for all (Alford & Niño, 2011).

Sources That Inform Equity in Mathematics

In spite of years of research, inequities still exist in U.S. mathematics classes. Wilkins and the Education Trust staff (2006) find that less than a third of African American high school students were exposed to college preparatory mathematics classes, and students of color including African Americans, Latinos, and Native Americans were twice as likely to be taught by inexperienced teachers. Access to a college preparatory mathematics curriculum has typically been restricted to a small group of students. The idea of tracking students into lower-level mathematics courses is a typical and ineffective school response to failed student performance.

Studies show that students who are placed into remedial courses receive instruction focused on procedural skills only, limiting students' ability to learn complex, engaging, and meaningful mathematics (Darling-Hammond, 2010)—the type of mathematics the CCSS require. Students historically identified as underperformers should have access to and be exposed to mathematics lessons that teach students to think critically and reason about the mathematics and make sense of what they are learning. If students are to have opportunities to be successful beyond high school, college- and career-preparatory mathematics can no longer be available to a select few. Whether students pursue postsecondary education or go directly into the workforce, richer college- and career-preparatory mathematics is a prerequisite (Achieve, 2005).

Doug Reeves's (2003) report on research from the Center for Performance Assessment on high-performing high-poverty schools dispels the myth that poverty and ethnicity are the only variables related to student learning. Over 90 percent of students met or exceeded academic achievement, determined by local assessments, despite 90 percent of the students receiving free and reduced lunch, and 90 percent or more being minority students. Reeves (2003) refers to these schools as *90-90-90 schools*. The following common themes emerged from these schools.

- Every work aspect of the school was focused on academic achievement.

- There were clear curriculum choices that emphasized the essential ideas of a subject in lieu of teaching every skill standard.

- Students' progress was effectively monitored weekly, and students had multiple opportunities to demonstrate understanding.

- There was a strong emphasis on nonfiction writing.

- Teachers collaboratively graded student work.

Katie Haycock (1998) examines schools that show academic gains for traditionally underperforming students. One study from Boston finds that consistent and excellent teaching in high school mathematics produced academic "gains on average that exceeded the national median (14.6 to 11.0 nationally) whereas the bottom third showed virtually no growth" (p. 8). Haycock's (Peske & Haycock, 2006) review on teacher effectiveness finds that schools with high-poverty or high-minority students were twice as likely to have mathematics teachers who were not mathematics majors.

Thus, differences in teacher quality and experience continue to affect student achievement, especially among diverse populations. Student success is predicated on teachers who have content and pedagogical expertise to meet students' learning needs. Using the data, the researchers identified qualities associated with high teacher effectiveness including strong verbal and mathematics skills, a deep of conceptual knowledge of mathematics, and strong pedagogical skills. These findings support Shulman's (1986) research on pedagogical content knowledge—high-quality teaching strongly correlates with robust instructional skills and content knowledge. His research frames the groundwork for shared teacher knowledge as part of a PLC expectation and verifies that the more pedagogical content knowledge a teacher has, the more mathematics students learn.

An important aspect of PLC leadership is your ability and willingness support to a coherent teacher-based response to resources and interventions that is the same for all students in the grade level or the course. This includes plans for addressing the needs of and reaching out to linguistically diverse students. Collaborative teams should ensure that high expectations are held for every student, regardless of race, language, socioeconomic status, or current proficiency level. To ensure students reach the high expectations of the Common Core State Standards for mathematics, your collaborative teams are required to orchestrate strong interventions and supports for each student in a course or grade level. In a professional learning community, you cannot allow teachers to provide response to intervention in isolation from one another.

And, as importantly, the team- and school-designed interventions *cannot* be optional for students. It is a moral imperative for teachers and teacher teams to monitor each student's individual progress toward meeting the learning targets of the unit and to require students to actively participate in the team's provided intervention response.

This moral imperative prevents teachers from opting out of providing students with the interventions the collaborative team identifies, and it prevents students from opting out as well, especially as students get older and into grades 6–12. Thus, every teacher of the collaborative team is held accountable to each student of the team. As a school leader, you are accountable for removing the barriers of time, funding, apathy, or intervention program quality (how students re-engage in the learning) that would prevent students from receiving necessary and timely interventions.

To move forward and commit to equity improvement, collaborative teams are reflective and purposeful when creating a plan for intervention and support. To meet the demands of the CCSS, you will need to model reflective behavior for your teams by using tools with them such as the one provided in table 5.2. You can complete the equity reflection activity in table 5.2 both individually and with teams, and then use it to focus areas of improvement in your overall school practices as it relates to equity.

Table 5.2: Equity Reflection Tool

Focused Area	Reflection Questions	Comments
Access	What process is used for mathematics placement into sixth- through twelfth-grade mathematics classes? Is it coherent in its application across schools? Do students have opportunities to advance through each grade with full proficiency in the expected CCSS grade-level standards? Are any groups of students denied access to college-preparatory or honors-level courses? How do you know and how do you monitor this?	
Grading	Is every team member's definition of an A, B, C, D, or F (or a standards-based report scale) the same? Does each team grade some portion of student assessment instruments together to ensure equitable grading? What is the quality of the feedback each teacher on the teacher team provides to students?	

continued →

Focused Area	Reflection Questions	Comments
Data-Driven Practices	Are data broken down by subpopulation to ensure the needs of each learner are met?	
	Does the team review the unit-by-unit student achievement data to inform instructional practices?	
	Are data collected on specific interventions and support to track and monitor effectiveness for student improvement?	
Task Selection	When planning a unit of instruction, do teacher teams develop common artifacts, tools, and representations of the standards in order to meet the learning needs of every student?	
	Does the team select or develop rich mathematical tasks with the appropriate assessing and advancing questions for each student to use?	
	Does the team identify essential prerequisite knowledge and skills needed for an upcoming unit of instruction?	
Assessments	Does the team use common grading rubrics for scoring all formative assessment instruments (tests and quizzes)?	
	Are assessments high quality and representative of the Common Core mathematics assessment expectations?	
	How are students involved in the teaching-assessing-learning cycle?	
Interventions and Support	Do teachers have time within the school day to collaborate on issues specific to student learning, students with disabilities, or English learners?	
	What team-level interventions are currently being offered for struggling students?	
	Are students required to attend the assigned team interventions if they do not meet expected learning standards?	

Visit **go.solution-tree.com/commoncore** for a reproducible version of this table.

As a school leader, you should use the reflection tool in table 5.2 as a beneficial tool for creating a schoolwide or districtwide commitment to pursue areas of inequity and to create a systematic process that ensures every child receives the additional time and support needed to learn mathematics at high levels. A PLC is committed to high standards of learning for each student.

Student Learning Needs for Success

The current reality of student knowledge and understanding should be used to inform teaching and learning. Assessment data can be used to drive instructional practices and inform teaching and learning to create an intentional *response to learning* during steps four and five of the assessment cycle. The data should not be used to place a student into lower-level mathematics experiences, which would perpetuate limited access to higher-level mathematics. In a PLC, the idea is to give the student a box to stand on so he or she can make it over the bar of expectations for the grade level or course. The solution should not be to lower the bar for that student.

Thus, students identified with learning gaps still have access to rich mathematics; they just have access with support. As a leader in a PLC, you enable collaborative teams to identify students' background knowledge, both mathematical and linguistic, to properly plan and support them (Fisher, Frey, & Rothenberg, 2011). Thus, as described in the teaching-assessing-learning cycle, your collaborative teams use student data for instructional purposes, *and* students use the data to self-assess their own mathematical knowledge and conceptual understanding that leads them to characterize their level of progress toward each learning target as described in chapter 4 (pages 91–92).

As the assessment cycle progresses, you should help your collaborative teams capture and interpret data that measure student growth on specific course standards. This scrutiny of monitoring is called *progress monitoring*, which is a repeated measure of academic performance. Progress monitoring will track current learning, and it is also used to chart students' growth progress to inform instruction of individual students (National Center for Response to Intervention [NCRTI], n.d.).

During steps two and five of the assessment cycle, you should ensure that each collaborative team collects multiple points of data to monitor and review students' progress throughout a unit of instruction (before, during, and after). To map individual student growth on each standard, collaborative teams can use formative in-class data as well as data collected from the assessment instruments used during the unit.

Your leadership role is to teach and lead the process of effective data analysis. You can use the checklist in table 5.3 (page 118) to help your teams identify specific data to be collected and analyzed to monitor students' progress. You should help each collaborative team review specific data weekly or with each unit of instruction; school- and district-level teams may review less frequently, depending on the essential questions in the table.

Table 5.3: High-Quality Data Checklist

Data Type	Essential Questions	What Data Can Answer This Question?	How Are Data Monitored? How Often?
Collaborative Teacher Teams			
Formative Data	What in-class formative assessment processes are used on a unit-by-unit basis to inform the teacher (and the team) about student learning?		
	Can we identify students (by name and need) who are not proficient?		
	How do we provide assessment feedback to students?		
	How are students expected to take action on the feedback?		
	How do we assist students with goal setting and with self-assessment of learning targets in need of *action*?		
Tasks	What are common student misconceptions for this learning target?		
	Is this a trend for all students or just a specific subpopulation?		
	What are the literacy demands of the student mathematical tasks we provide?		
Intervention	What interventions are provided in class as well as outside the class?		
	How many students are attending the intervention, and is it required?		
	How frequent is the intervention?		
	How is the intervention deemed to be successful for students?		
Schoolwide or Districtwide Teams			
Summative Data	What percent of students are achieving As, Bs, and Cs?		
	What percent of students are receiving Ds and Fs?		
	What percent of students are meeting the standards at the elementary level?		

Data Type	Essential Questions	What Data Can Answer This Question?	How Are Data Monitored? How Often?
Schoolwide or Districtwide Teams			
Summative Data (continued)	What percent of students are not meeting the standards at the elementary level?		
	What percent of students are not proficient on the assessment instruments we use?		
	Are there defined benchmark assessment content standard clusters that are not being met by the students?		
Accessibility	What is the student percentage participation rate in each course by subgroup?		
	What percent of students at each grade level are enrolled in college preparatory courses?		
	At the elementary level, are there any below-grade-level mathematics courses?		
Attendance	Do varying levels of attendance affect grade-distribution rates? How do you know?		

Visit **go.solution-tree.com/commoncore** for a reproducible version of this table.

In a PLC, your collaborative teams should decide what data to analyze to assess students' knowledge and determine the effectiveness of their work, but they may need your guidance for how to do so. What data will let them know they are achieving short-term wins with their students? The decisions about data use will define the clear, nondiscretionary, and collaborative teacher actions needed for student success. Your teams may wish to pursue more information about specific data dialogue prompts or questions to ask while reviewing data. (Visit www.allthingsplc.info and search the Tools & Resources for more information about specific data and dialogue prompts to ask while reviewing data.)

Recall that when collaborative teams reflect on the four critical questions of a PLC, the answers drive the work of the collaborative teams (DuFour et al., 2008). The four questions are:

1. What are the knowledge, skills, and dispositions we want all students to acquire as a result of their experience in our course or grade level?

2. How will we know each student has acquired the intended knowledge, skills, and dispositions? What is our process for gathering information on each student's proficiency?

3. How will our teams and school respond to students who experience difficulty in acquiring the intended knowledge and skills? How will we provide them with additional time and support for learning in a way that is timely, directive, precise, and systematic?

4. How will our teams and school provide additional enrichment for students who are already proficient?

To meet the demands of the CCSS, create equity, and access rich mathematics, collaborative teams must be especially attentive to address and answer these last two questions through their response to intervention structures.

The PLC Required Response to Learning

As a school leader, you must make certain that increasing access to the rich mathematics of the CCSS will not lead to increased failure (Seeley, 2009). In the pursuit of equity, your goal is to provide access to rich mathematics for all students and to foster teachers' awareness and acceptance of this goal. However, you cannot raise standards and expectations without identifying appropriate support for students not meeting these standards. The teachers' responses to the needs of students who are not meeting the standards must be purposefully planned, universal for all students, timely, and well communicated. The purpose of intentional responses is to provide clarity for all stakeholders—including students, teachers, parents, administrators, and community members—about what is valued, what is assessed, and the progress of each student toward learning the Common Core mathematics content. These intentional responses to intervention are *nondiscretionary* for establishing equity and access.

To create a successful response to learning, your efforts will ensure that your collaborative teams will embrace the need to pursue equity, be reflective about current instructional practices, clearly identify students who are not being successful with mathematics, and be able to brainstorm all the potential resources teachers might use for students who are struggling. Only then are teachers ready to evaluate the effectiveness of the current interventions (Buffum, Mattos, & Weber, 2008).

According to National Center on Response to Intervention (n.d.), RTI is a system that "integrates research-based practices, progress monitoring, and required support and is a systematic approach for improved teaching and learning" (p. 4). Buffum, Mattos, and Weber (2010) further state that RTI's "underlying premise is that schools should not wait until students fall far enough behind to qualify for special education" (p. 10).

RTI was part of the reauthorization of the Individuals With Disabilities Education Improvement Act (IDEIA) in 2004, so some schools view RTI as a requirement or as a way to identify students with special needs. RTI is not just about identifying special education students. The RTI framework can assist with defining how you create equity in your mathematics program. Teachers' response to learning can utilize this framework to assist with creating equity and access for each student.

To reach the desired outcomes of the CCSS, teachers need to recognize that some students may require additional support and intervention beyond what is typically provided in class. Your leadership will be instrumental in enabling teachers to meet the requirements of this aspect of the CCSS. Although all public schools are required to have an RTI plan, Johnson, Smith, and Harris (2009) highlight the differences in the purpose of RTI at the elementary and secondary level. At the elementary level, RTI is used to:

- Screen to identify at-risk students

- Provide early interventions to supplement the general curriculum

- Use student interventions as part of disability determination

At the secondary level, the purpose of RTI is focused on:

- Building the capacity of all learners

- Meeting the demands of diverse student populations

- Increasing graduation rate

- Using researched best practices for increased learning

RTI is a model for comprehensive school reform aimed intentionally at increasing student achievement. The RTI framework enables all students to be successful in elementary, middle, and high school, which in turn supports schools as they progress in their continuous improvement plans (Johnson et al., 2009). While there are many forms of RTI, for the purpose of this book, the RTI framework referenced has three tiers.

Tier 1: What Is Your Differentiated Response to Learning?

Tier 1 instruction, research-affirmed practices designed to meet the needs of each learner, is the core of the RTI model and addresses the expected student outcomes. During this first stage of RTI, supports are provided to every student. Fisher et al. (2011) suggest that "interventions are an element of good teaching" (p. 2), and these interventions begin in the classroom. Therefore, it is imperative your collaborative teams focus their work on meaningful and rigorous mathematical tasks delivered with high-quality instruction. Tier 1 instruction is the first line of defense for struggling students and can include but is not limited to:

- High-quality, researched-based instructional practices

- Differentiated instruction

- Screening and use of multiple assessment measures to monitor students' progress (Bender & Crane, 2011)

- Guided instruction with scaffolding and modeling that integrates listening, speaking, writing, and reading for ELs

- Language-acquisition intervention that supports learning of both content and language (Fisher et al., 2011)

In Tier 1, collaborative teams start by making sure every student has access to rigorous mathematics content, high-quality instruction, support, and necessary interventions. Teachers' *differentiated* response to learning will be required to ensure that all students are learning.

Wormeli (2006) states, "Differentiation is doing what is fair for students" (p. 3). *Fair* does not mean having the same learning experience. Differentiation requires teacher teams to make adjustments and do things differently for individual students. Teachers do this regularly without being explicit about what they are differentiating. Some students receive preferential seating to see the board, some students get extended time for tests, and some are challenged to think of other ways to solve a problem because teachers know they can explore a concept more deeply than their classmates or from a different point of view. The advancing and assessing questions in figure 2.12 (page 53) are a way to differentiate small-group peer-to-peer discussions. These are all basic examples of differentiation.

Buffum, Mattos, and Weber (2012) state, "Prevention is the best intervention" (p. 61). As part of Tier 1 differentiated instruction, teachers need to assess students' prior knowledge necessary to master the new standard. Using a common formative assessment measuring prerequisite knowledge during the assessment cycle will help you plan preventative scaffolding and support for students. (Figure 2.12, page 53, provides a section on beginning-of-class routines and asks how the warm-up activity connects to student prior knowledge.)

Within the RTI framework, differentiation is explicit and is purposefully planned using a compilation of research-informed practices to maximize student achievement starting with Tier 1. Your collaborative teams use formative assessment data and knowledge of students' prior knowledge, language, and diverse cultures to offer students in the same class different teaching and learning opportunities to address their learning needs.

By using differentiation strategies, teams are not making the content easier; they are making the content *accessible*. As a leader, this is a critical point for you to emphasize to teachers, as many of them will view differentiated instruction as "watering down the curriculum." Your collaborative teams need to plan for differentiation by developing tasks that allow students multiple points of entry. With your teams, reflect on the prompts in table 5.4. Use this tool to analyze the ways in which your teacher teams ensure they are planning for differentiation.

Table 5.4: Tool for the Teacher Team Differentiated Response to Task Learning

Questions to Consider	Reflection
What is the learning target for all, for some, or for few? What is the expected level of mastery of the standard?	
Does this task give opportunities for different student readiness levels as part of their task planning?	

Questions to Consider	Reflection
Are there multiple ways to help students make sense of the mathematics for this standard?	
How can the task be adjusted to challenge students more deeply if needed?	
Can the task be adjusted to increase access to students who are still struggling with background or prior knowledge?	

Visit **go.solution-tree.com/commoncore** for a reproducible version of this table.

Differentiated instruction is about providing students tools to problem solve and make meaning of the mathematics, at whatever learning level appropriate. This reflection activity will once again help the teacher team to focus on whether their task selection and instruction of those tasks meet the needs of all learners. How effectively your teams use differentiated practices to create access and equity will ultimately go a long way in determining how much students learn (Wormeli, 2006). (Visit www.caroltomlinson .com/otherresources.html and www.ascd.org/research-a-topic/differentiated-instruction -resources.aspx for more differentiation resources.)

Tier 2: What Is Your Targeted Response to Learning?

Tier 2 interventions are directed more toward specific Common Core mathematics skills or understanding of learning standards and will include academic and behavioral interventions. Tier 2 interventions are more intensive and targeted for students who continue to struggle even after Tier 1 differentiated instruction is shown to be ineffective. Tier 2 interventions are supplemental and not intended for each student. Examples of Tier 2 interventions include (Fisher et al., 2011):

- Increased frequency and duration of interventions

- Small-group instruction

- Additional instructional time outside of the regular mathematics class

- Intensive development of language proficiency to develop content knowledge

To generate a *targeted* response to learning, Tier 2 requires intensive progress monitoring as a means to clearly identify students' learning gaps. Ongoing formative assessment of student progress toward identified learning standards aligned to the unit or chapter enables customized additional support for targeted students. Step three of the assessment cycle (figure 4.2, page 90) also requires students to take action on feedback and is a tool for engaging students in Tier 2 strategies.

Additional mathematics support and interventions in Tier 2 should look significantly different from the first learning experience. You should ask your teams, "Is the learning experience significantly different in order to increase the likelihood of student re-engagement and improved achievement with the standard?" As your teams reflect about instructional strategies, they will need to determine which instructional strategies are most effective. Students who are in need of Tier 2 interventions do not need more of the same thing (Buffum et al., 2008). The *targeted* intervention—whether it be in an after-school program, a special-assigned support period, or before-school session—needs to provide the student with an opportunity for action on the specific learning target gaps as the gaps occur.

Tier 3: What Is Your Intensive Response to Learning?

Tier 3 interventions are intensive in nature as students who need these interventions usually have multiple needs. Tier 3 interventions are greater in intensity with increasing frequency and duration (Buffum et al., 2008). Interventions at this stage can include, but are not limited to, placement into inclusion classrooms, one-on-one tutoring, or specific learning and behavioral interventions (Johnson et al., 2009). The intensive assistance is in addition to classroom instruction, not in lieu of classroom instruction. Your teams' role in Tier 3 intervention is to continually monitor each student's progress and increase the amount of time and frequency of the interventions. The *intensive* response to learning should be individualized and based on addressing multiple academic and behavioral needs.

A Major Paradigm Shift in Mathematics Intervention Practices

The CCSS require a shift in how your collaborative teams respond to learning, realizing that interventions are no longer optional. To guarantee equity for each student, your leadership should indicate that interventions at any tier cannot be optional for K–12 students. In a PLC culture, you ensure that the collaborative teams implement a *required response to intervention* (R²TI) for mathematics.

When students are struggling, their typical response to academic challenges is to retreat from the challenge, become nonparticipants in their learning, passively engage in the classwork, or ultimately drop out of school. Buffum et al. (2008) say, "As adults, we understand the long-term consequences of educational failure far better than our students do. We should never allow them to embark upon that path" (p. 62). To effectively implement the RTI framework, your leadership efforts and those of collaborative teams, schools, and the district should be focused on how to require interventions at every tier, hence R²TI.

When identifying interventions, you need to ensure your collaborative teams are intentional about the requirements of R²TI. According to Johnson et al. (2009), "RTI as a systems framework has the potential to coordinate various programs so that they work in concert with one another to achieve the desired outcomes" (p. 17). For the R²TI model to impact student achievement, your collaborative teams should identify required interventions based on data and individual needs. By requiring interventions, school improvement efforts will not be destroyed by dwindling support or misunderstanding of the purpose.

Use table 5.5 as a diagnostic tool with your teams to identify current interventions or strategies being implemented in your school or district to support struggling students and to articulate how all stakeholders monitor the interventions.

Table 5.5: School and District Intervention Reflection Questions

What Initiatives Are You Utilizing to Meet the Varying Needs of Students?	Who Is Responsible for the Intervention?	What Is the Current Level of Success of Each Subpopulation Participating in the Intervention?	What Data Are Being Reviewed to Monitor Students' Progress?	Which Students Are Participating in the Collaborative Team's Interventions?

Visit **go.solution-tree.com/commoncore** for a reproducible version of this table.

As you consider the responses for table 5.5, what percent of students needing intervention are actually attending the support programs? To ensure academic achievement for each learner, students must be required to participate in interventions. Opening an extra support class or offering after-school tutoring is good but not sufficient. If students are to meet the challenges of the CCSS learning targets, you and your collaborative teams need to establish systematic interventions as part of the R²TI plan. Your collaborative teams need to be intentional and purposeful regarding student access and movement in and out of the R²TI programs.

As your schoolwide leadership team determines appropriate interventions, you should ensure that academic intervention is not a *happenstance* opportunity. The teams' response to each student's learning must address the following questions.

- Is the intervention needed on an individual basis, or does the gap exist in all students or particular subpopulations?

- Do students need differentiated instruction from their teachers (Tier 1) or targeted intervention from the school and collaborative teams (Tier 2)?

- Is the intervention tailored to meet the needs of a specific subpopulation?

- For ELs, what research-based best practices for content literacy are being used?

- For inclusion students, what accommodations or modifications are being implemented to differentiate learning?

- What responsive teaching is needed for all students to be successful?

Tier 1 differentiated instruction for ELs requires creating a gradual release model of instruction (Fisher et al., 2011). Although specific for ELs, the intent of the interventions is about developing prerequisite language and literacy skills to effectively support students learning the mathematics detailed in the CCSS. For students who have little or no literacy skills, either in English or their primary language, collaborative teams should plan for building student responsibility into the learning experiences. Fisher et al. (2011) suggest several teaching strategies to prepare students for a specific task:

- Tap into prior knowledge.

- Set clear learning targets.

- Explain and model the concept (I do, we do, you do).

- Create a visual representation of the expected learning.

- Focus on building academic language and vocabulary.

- Provide examples and nonexamples.

The skills needed to develop language proficiency—listening, speaking, reading, and writing—are all essential components to developing students' mathematical understanding.

Your collaborative teams should discuss what is working instructionally, what is not working, and how utilizing effective instructional strategies is impacting student achievement. To answer the critical questions of a PLC, you will need to focus your efforts continuously through the assessment cycle.

Use table 5.6 to begin planning your school or district's intentional *response to learning* within each tier. This planning tool provides reflection questions about current interventions and identifies opportunities to improve your current R²TI framework. (Refer to table 5.5, page 125, for your current list of interventions.)

Table 5.6: Tier 1, Tier 2, or Tier 3 Diagnostic Tool

	Diagnostic Question	Comments
Student Needs	What Tier 1, Tier 2, or Tier 3 interventions are needed?	
	What data are we using to support this claim?	
	How do teams support students from special populations (students with disabilities or ELs)?	
	What professional development is needed for team members?	
Tier 1: Differentiated Response to Learning	What type of differentiated instruction do team members implement?	
	What accommodations or modifications are being implemented?	
	Do team members identify language barriers to student learning?	
	What language proficiency issues are team members addressing?	

	Diagnostic Question	Comments
Tier 2: Targeted Response to Learning	How will teams increase the intensity of interventions?	
	What small-group instruction do teachers need to provide?	
	What is the intensive development of language proficiency needed?	
Tier 3: Intensive Response to Learning	What is the current schedule of intensive support?	
	What is the current frequency of that support?	
	Are there academic and behavioral interventions needed for the students?	
Evidence	How are students placed and required to participate in the intervention?	
Implementation	Who will be responsible for implementing the support?	
	What evidence does the team need to monitor implementation success?	
	What support from administration or other personnel is needed to sustain the intervention?	
Accountability	What data will be used to determine intervention effectiveness?	

Visit **go.solution-tree.com/commoncore** for a reproducible version of this table.

Once you help your collaborative teams accept the responsibility to meet the needs of each learner, conversations are no longer centered on trivial items that have little or no impact on student achievement. Conversations are about learning experiences, equitable instructional practices, and cognitive-demand tasks that meet the vision of the CCSS for mathematics. As teams focus on these nondiscretionary actions of a PLC, you will build the capacity of team members and increase shared knowledge of how best to meet the needs of all students.

Your Intentional R²TI for Learning

After your collaborative teams plan for student intervention and support, they should communicate their plan to you for monitoring students within each R²TI tier. Mathematics programs struggle severely with managing interventions if they do not specify how students are engaged within each intervention (Johnson et al., 2009). How will students move in and out of specific interventions? Your collaborative teams need to communicate what data are going to be used, specify the interventions that will meet specific academic needs, and identify resources needed to support each intervention. In addition, collaborative teams must assess the impact of academic interventions to measure their effectiveness.

Table 5.7 is a valuable planning template and tool to assist with developing your R²TI model.

Table 5.7: Intervention Planning Tool

Intervention	Tier	What Students Need Intervention?	How Often Do Students Get Support?	How Will Students Receive Intervention?

Visit **go.solution-tree.com/commoncore** for a reproducible version of this table.

Kanold (2011a) identifies three levels of teams needed for continuous school improvement.

1. A district-level team for continuous improvement of all districtwide programs

2. A school-level principal- or school-site-leader-led team for continuous improvement of school-based programs

3. Grade-level or course-based teacher-led teams for continuous improvement of student achievement

To support R²TI, school leaders like you must work with teacher teams to develop and support an infrastructure that will effectively monitor and continuously adjust student interventions. With shared leadership and a PLC culture, district and school leaders develop support teams that monitor one specific aspect of R²TI. Whether it is the intervention team, support team, data team, screening team, or assessment team, it is imperative that R²TI is a collaborative effort capitalizing on informative data and identifying tiered interventions necessary to enable each student to learn mathematics well. (Visit www.allthingsplc.info, and search for "RTI" or "PRTI" to learn about several RTI models. Also, visit **go.solution-tree.com/commoncore** for the online-only reproducible "Diagnostic Tool for Tier 2 Targeted Interventions.")

Looking Ahead

To create an equitable mathematics program, leaders, administrators, and teachers should work together to ensure that the current processes and the R²TI framework create access and equity for each student. The focus of this chapter was to define equity and to design a reflective path and an intentional plan through the R²TI framework for establishing equitable access to mathematics learning for each student. Collaborative teams ensure students have equitable learning environments, which includes curriculum, instruction, and assessment, within a supportive R²TI framework. Collaborative teams with a vision for equity and a fully developed R²TI model in place to monitor student achievement will make certain the needs of each student are being met. Your collaborative pursuit of a positive, richly embedded, and *required* RTI system for each student will not be easy. However, it will be so worthwhile as you pursue the social justice and equitable opportunities to ensure a level mathematics playing field for the learning of every child in your school or district.

Chapter 5 Extending My Understanding

1. Refer to your reflections in tables 5.1 (page 112) and 5.2 (page 115). What is your current reality of equitable learning experiences? What leadership responsibilities must you pursue to achieve equity?

2. Refer to table 5.3 (page 118). What data do you have or what data do you need to effectively monitor students' CCSS learning? How will you use these data with your collaborative teams?

3. Think about Tier 1 differentiated instruction (pages 121–123). What is your differentiated response to learning? How are your collaborative teams making the content accessible for each student?

4. What do your current *targeted* Tier 2 interventions look like? Are they required for all students not meeting current performance standards on a unit-by-unit basis? How would or should you change the process students follow to access the intervention and re-engagement into learning the standards? Is additional instructional time provided to students who need it?

5. Refer to the three levels of teacher-led teams—district, school, or grade-level or course-based. What teams do you have in your school or district, and what level of support is provided for implementing the R²TI framework? How does the work of each team support vision for equity and access to rich mathematics?

6. As you develop your R²TI framework, what are your next steps as a leader for ensuring collaborative teams implement it with fidelity? What are your current strengths? What will be your challenges? What additional support or professional development will be needed to solidify your collaborative teams' response to learning?

Online Resources

Visit **go.solution-tree.com/commoncore** for links to these resources.

- **RTI Action Network for High School (www.rtinetwork.org/high-school):** The RTI Action Network is dedicated to the effective implementation of RTI in U.S. school districts. This website offers specific high school research, strategies for tiered interventions, and tools for implementation.

- **Classroom-Focused Improvement Process (School Improvement in Maryland, 2010; http://mdk12.org/process/cfip):** The Classroom-Focused Improvement Process is a six-step process for increasing student achievement that teachers plan and carry out during grade-level or cross-level team meetings as a part of their regular lesson-planning cycle.

- **National Center on Response to Intervention (www.rti4success.org):** This site provides a wealth of resources to plan, implement, and screen RTI, including professional development modules that teacher learning teams can use to initiate or improve a RTI program in schools, districts, or states.

- **Mathematics Leadership Resources (www.mathedleadership.org):** The National Council of Supervisors of Mathematics is an organization that assists mathematics educators in interpreting and understanding the CCSS to support the development and implementation of comprehensive, coherent instruction and assessment systems.

- **RTI books and reproducibles (go.solution-tree.com/rti):** This site offers free reproducibles and numerous resources on RTI, including resources from *Simplifying Response to Intervention: Four Essential Guiding Principles* (Buffum et al., 2012).

EPILOGUE

Your Mathematics Professional Development Model

Implementing the Common Core State Standards for mathematics presents you with both new challenges and new opportunities. The unprecedented adoption of a common set of mathematics standards by nearly every state provides the opportunity for U.S. educators to press the reset button on mathematics education (Larson, 2011). Collectively, you and your colleagues have the opportunity to rededicate yourselves to ensuring that all students are provided with exemplary teaching and learning experiences, with access to the supports necessary to guarantee an opportunity for improved mathematical proficiency.

The CCSS college and career aspirations and vision for teaching, learning, and assessing students usher in an opportunity for unprecedented implementation of research-informed practices in your school or district's mathematics program. In order to meet the expectations of the five fundamental paradigm shifts described in this book, you will want to assess your current practice and reality as a school against the roadmap to implementation described in figure E.1.

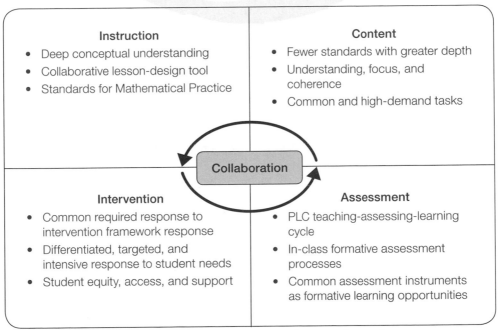

Figure E.1: PLCs at Work implementing Common Core mathematics.

Visit **go.solution-tree.com/commoncore** for a reproducible version of this figure.

Figure E.1 describes the essential paradigm shifts for your collaborative teams' instruction, content, assessment, and intervention necessary for your mathematics program to support teacher understanding and student acquisition of the Common Core.

As you professionally develop the work of each member of your various collaborative teams, remember that the goal is to prepare teachers and students for the expectations of the Common Core mathematics standards, the Mathematical Practices, and the assessments. College and career readiness is a goal for all K–12 students—whether your state is part of the CCSS or not. As a school mathematics leader, you must ensure teachers and students pursue and sustain this goal.

Each sector in figure E.1 describes three vital collaborative team behaviors for that area of change. If you hope to break through any current areas of student and teacher stagnation in your mathematics program and achieve greater student success than ever before, then these paradigms provide part of your mindset for never-ending change, growth, and improvement within the reasoning and conceptual understanding focus of the mathematics instruction your students deserve and must receive in your school or district.

We wrote this book because during professional development, we often hear from teachers, "You need to share this information with our administrators! We need their support!" So we chose to provide you with the same message about change that is in each of the grade-level books.

At the same time, we often hear, "Please help our teachers to better understand and deliver on the message you are giving us!" So the grade-level books provide a deeper support to the important work of your teams that you are expected to lead.

As the Common Core story unfolds in your school or district, there will be a thousand voices telling you what to do. We hope this book and the books in the series will help you to cut through all of the noise and allow you to just focus on doing a few things really well. Think: one paradigm at a time! If you already have the benefit of working as a PLC, you are well on your way to that equity pursuit: "Ready, Set, Action!" We wish you the best and invite you to contact us anytime to let us know your story, your concerns, and your triumphs! Thank you for considering this book as your professional development resource in mathematics.

Standards for Mathematical Practice

Source: NGA & CCSSO, 2010, pp. 6–8. © Copyright 2010. National Governors Association Center for Best Practices and Council of Chief State School Officers. All rights reserved. Used with permission.

The Standards for Mathematical Practice describe varieties of expertise that mathematics educators at all levels should seek to develop in their students. These practices rest on important "processes and proficiencies" with longstanding importance in mathematics education. The first of these are the NCTM process standards of problem solving, reasoning and proof, communication, representation, and connections. The second are the strands of mathematical proficiency specified in the National Research Council's report *Adding It Up:* adaptive reasoning, strategic competence, conceptual understanding (comprehension of mathematical concepts, operations and relations), procedural fluency (skill in carrying out procedures flexibly, accurately, efficiently and appropriately), and productive disposition (habitual inclination to see mathematics as sensible, useful, and worthwhile, coupled with a belief in diligence and one's own efficacy).

1. Make sense of problems and persevere in solving them. Mathematically proficient students start by explaining to themselves the meaning of a problem and looking for entry points to its solution. They analyze givens, constraints, relationships, and goals. They make conjectures about the form and meaning of the solution and plan a solution pathway rather than simply jumping into a solution attempt. They consider analogous problems, and try special cases and simpler forms of the original problem in order to gain insight into its solution. They monitor and evaluate their progress and change course if necessary. Older students might, depending on the context of the problem, transform algebraic expressions or change the viewing window on their graphing calculator to get the information they need. Mathematically proficient students can explain correspondences between equations, verbal descriptions, tables, and graphs or draw diagrams of important features and relationships, graph data, and search for regularity or trends. Younger students might rely on using concrete objects or pictures to help conceptualize and solve a problem. Mathematically proficient students check their answers to problems using a different method, and they continually ask themselves, "Does this make sense?" They can understand the approaches of others to solving complex problems and identify correspondences between different approaches.

2. Reason abstractly and quantitatively. Mathematically proficient students make sense of quantities and their relationships in problem situations. They bring two complementary abilities to bear on problems involving quantitative relationships: the ability to decontextualize—to abstract a given situation and represent it symbolically and manipulate the representing symbols as if they have a life of their own, without necessarily attending to their referents—and the ability to contextualize, to pause as needed during the manipulation process in order to probe into the referents for the symbols involved. Quantitative reasoning entails habits of creating a coherent representation of the problem at hand; considering the units involved; attending to the meaning of quantities, not just how to compute them; and knowing and flexibly using different properties of operations and objects.

3. Construct viable arguments and critique the reasoning of others. Mathematically proficient students understand and use stated assumptions, definitions, and previously established results in constructing arguments. They make conjectures and build a logical progression of statements to explore the truth of their conjectures. They are able to analyze situations by breaking them into cases, and can recognize and use counterexamples. They justify their conclusions, communicate them to others, and respond to the arguments of others. They reason inductively about data, making plausible arguments that take into account the context from which the data arose. Mathematically proficient students are also able to compare the effectiveness of two plausible arguments, distinguish correct logic or reasoning from that which is flawed, and—if there is a flaw in an argument—explain what it is. Elementary students can construct arguments using concrete referents such as objects, drawings, diagrams, and actions. Such arguments can make sense and be correct, even though they are not generalized or made formal until later grades. Later, students learn to determine domains to which an argument applies. Students at all grades can listen or read the arguments of others, decide whether they make sense, and ask useful questions to clarify or improve the arguments.

4. Model with mathematics. Mathematically proficient students can apply the mathematics they know to solve problems arising in everyday life, society, and the workplace. In early grades, this might be as simple as writing an addition equation to describe a situation. In middle grades, a student might apply proportional reasoning to plan a school event or analyze a problem in the community. By high school, a student might use geometry to solve a design problem or use a function to describe how one quantity of interest depends on another. Mathematically proficient students who can apply what they know are comfortable making assumptions and approximations to simplify a complicated situation, realizing that these may need revision later. They are able to identify important quantities in a practical situation and map their relationships using such tools as diagrams, two-way tables, graphs, flowcharts and formulas. They can analyze those relationships mathematically to draw conclusions. They routinely interpret their mathematical results in the context of the situation and reflect on whether the results make sense, possibly improving the model if it has not served its purpose.

5. Use appropriate tools strategically. Mathematically proficient students consider the available tools when solving a mathematical problem. These tools might include pencil and paper, concrete models, a ruler, a protractor, a calculator, a spreadsheet, a computer algebra system, a statistical package, or dynamic geometry software. Proficient students are sufficiently familiar with tools appropriate for their grade or course to make sound decisions about when each of these tools might be helpful, recognizing both the insight to be gained and their limitations. For example, mathematically proficient high school students analyze graphs of functions and solutions generated using a graphing calculator. They detect possible errors by strategically using estimation and other mathematical knowledge. When making mathematical models, they know that technology can enable them to visualize the results of varying assumptions, explore consequences, and compare predictions with data. Mathematically proficient students at various grade levels are able to identify relevant external mathematical resources, such as digital content located on a website, and use them to pose or solve problems. They are able to use technological tools to explore and deepen their understanding of concepts.

6. Attend to precision. Mathematically proficient students try to communicate precisely to others. They try to use clear definitions in discussion with others and in their own reasoning. They state the meaning of the symbols they choose, including using the equal sign consistently and appropriately. They are careful about specifying units of measure, and labeling axes to clarify the correspondence with quantities in a problem. They calculate accurately and efficiently, express numerical answers with a degree of precision appropriate for the problem context. In the elementary grades, students give carefully formulated explanations to each other. By the time they reach high school they have learned to examine claims and make explicit use of definitions.

7. Look for and make use of structure. Mathematically proficient students look closely to discern a pattern or structure. Young students, for example, might notice that three and seven more is the same amount as seven and three more, or they may sort a collection of shapes according to how many sides the shapes have. Later, students will see 7×8 equals the well remembered $7 \times 5 + 7 \times 3$, in preparation for learning about the distributive property. In the expression $x^2 + 9x + 14$, older students can see the 14 as 2×7 and the 9 as $2 + 7$. They recognize the significance of an existing line in a geometric figure and can use the strategy of drawing an auxiliary line for solving problems. They also can step back for an overview and shift perspective. They can see complicated things, such as some algebraic expressions, as single objects or as being composed of several objects. For example, they can see $5 - 3(x - y)^2$ as 5 minus a positive number times a square and use that to realize that its value cannot be more than 5 for any real numbers x and y.

8. Look for and express regularity in repeated reasoning. Mathematically proficient students notice if calculations are repeated, and look both for general methods and for shortcuts. Upper elementary students might notice when dividing 25 by 11 that they are repeating the same calculations over and over again, and conclude they have a repeating decimal. By paying attention to the calculation of slope as they repeatedly check whether points are on the line through (1, 2) with slope 3, middle school students might abstract the equation $(y - 2)/(x - 1) = 3$. Noticing the regularity in the way terms cancel when expanding $(x - 1)(x + 1)$, $(x - 1)(x^2 + x + 1)$, and $(x - 1)(x^3 + x^2 + x + 1)$ might lead them to the general formula for the sum of a geometric series. As they work to solve a problem, mathematically proficient students maintain oversight of the process, while attending to the details. They continually evaluate the reasonableness of their intermediate results.

Connecting the Standards for Mathematical Practice to the Standards for Mathematical Content

The Standards for Mathematical Practice describe ways in which developing student practitioners of the discipline of mathematics increasingly ought to engage with the subject matter as they grow in mathematical maturity and expertise throughout the elementary, middle and high school years. Designers of curricula, assessments, and professional development should all attend to the need to connect the mathematical practices to mathematical content in mathematics instruction.

The Standards for Mathematical Content are a balanced combination of procedure and understanding. Expectations that begin with the word "understand" are often especially good opportunities to connect the practices to the content. Students who lack understanding of a topic may rely on procedures too heavily. Without a flexible base from which to work, they may be less likely to consider analogous problems, represent problems coherently, justify conclusions, apply the mathematics to practical situations, use technology mindfully to work with the mathematics, explain the mathematics accurately to other students, step back for an overview, or deviate from a known procedure to find a shortcut. In short, a lack of understanding effectively prevents a student from engaging in the mathematical practices.

In this respect, those content standards which set an expectation of understanding are potential "points of intersection" between the Standards for Mathematical Content and the Standards for Mathematical Practice. These points of intersection are intended to be weighted toward central and generative concepts in the school mathematics curriculum that most merit the time, resources, innovative energies, and focus necessary to qualitatively improve the curriculum, instruction, assessment, professional development, and student achievement in mathematics.

References and Resources

Achieve. (2005). *Rising to the challenge: Are high school graduates prepared for college and work?* Washington, DC: Author.

Achieve. (2010). *On the road to implementation.* Accessed at www.achieve.org/files/CCSSComm &Outreach.pdf on December 19, 2011.

Ainsworth, L. (2007). Common formative assessments: The centerpiece of an integrated standards-based grading system. In D. Reeves (Ed.), *Ahead of the curve: The power of assessment to transform teaching and learning* (pp. 79–102). Bloomington, IN: Solution Tree Press.

Alford, B., & Niño, M. (2011). *Leading academic achievement for English language learners: A guide for principals.* Thousand Oaks, CA: Corwin Press.

AllThingsPLC. (n.d.). *Making time for collaboration.* Accessed at www.allthingsplc.info/pdf /articles/MakingTimeforCollaboration.pdf on December 20, 2011.

Baccellieri, P. (2010). *Professional learning communities: Using data in decision making to improve student learning.* Huntington Beach, CA: Shell Education.

Ball, D. L., & Bass, H. (2003). Making mathematics reasonable in school. In J. Kilpatrick, W. G. Martin, & D. Schifter (Eds.), *A research companion to principles and standards for school mathematics* (pp. 27–44). Reston, VA: National Council of Teachers of Mathematics.

Barber, M., & Mourshed, M. (2007). *How the world's best performing school systems come out on top.* Accessed at http://mckinseyonsociety.com/downloads/reports/Education/Worlds _School_Systems_Final.pdf on December 19, 2011.

Barth, R. S. (2001). *Learning by heart.* San Francisco: Jossey-Bass.

Barth, R. S. (2006). Improving relationships within the schoolhouse. *Educational Leadership, 63*(6), 8–13.

Battista, M. T. (2008). Development of the Shape Makers geometry microworld: Design principles and research. In G. Blume & K. Heid (Eds.), *Research on technology in the learning and teaching of mathematics: Cases and perspectives* (Vol. 2, pp. 131–156). Charlotte, NC: National Council of Teachers of Mathematics & Information Age.

Bender, W. N., & Crane, D. (2011). *RTI in math: Practical guidelines for elementary teachers.* Bloomington, IN: Solution Tree Press.

Blank, R. K., de las Alas, N., & Smith, C. (2007). *Analysis of the quality of professional development programs for mathematics and science teachers: Findings from a cross-state study.* Washington, DC: Council of Chief State School Officers. Accessed at http://programs .ccsso.org/content/pdfs/Year_2_IMPDE_Fall_06_Rpt_with_errata-041708.pdf on December 19, 2011.

Bowgren, L., & Sever, K. (2010). *Differentiated professional development in a professional learning community.* Bloomington, IN: Solution Tree Press.

Boykin, A., & Noguera, P. (2011). *Creating the opportunity to learn*. Alexandria, VA: Association for Supervision and Curriculum Development.

Brown v. Board of Educ., 347 U.S. 483 (1954).

Brown, S., Seidelmann, T., & Zimmermann, G. (2006). *In the trenches: Three teacher's perspectives on moving beyond the math wars*. Accessed at http://mathematicallysane.com /in-the-trenches on July 1, 2011.

Buffum, A., Mattos, M., & Weber, C. (2008). *Pyramid response to intervention: RTI, professional learning communities, and how to respond when kids don't learn*. Bloomington, IN: Solution Tree Press.

Buffum, A., Mattos, M., & Weber, C. (2010). The why behind RTI. *Educational Leadership, 68*(2), 10–16.

Buffum, A., Mattos, M., & Weber, C. (2012). *Simplifying response to intervention: Four essential guiding principles*. Bloomington, IN: Solution Tree Press.

Burke, K. (2010). *Balanced assessment: From formative to summative*. Bloomington, IN: Solution Tree Press.

Bush, W. S., Briars, D. J., Confrey, J., Cramer, K., Lee, C., Martin, W. G., et al. (2011). *Common Core State Standards (CCSS) mathematics curriculum materials analysis project*. Accessed at www.mathedleadership.org/docs/ccss/CCSSO%20Mathematics%20Curriculum %20Analysis%20Project.Whole%20Document.6.1.11.Final.docx on November 15, 2011.

Canady, R. L., & Hotchkiss, P. R. (1989). It's a good score, just a bad grade! *Phi Delta Kappan, 71*(1), 68–71.

Cazden, C. (2001). *Classroom discourse: The language of teaching and learning*. Portsmouth, NH: Heinemann.

Chapin, S. H., & O'Connor, C. (2007). Academically productive talk: Supporting students' learning in mathematics. In W. G. Martin, M. Strutchens, & P. Elliot (Eds.), *The learning of mathematics* (pp. 113–139). Reston, VA: National Council of Teachers of Mathematics.

Cobb, P. (2000). Conducting teaching experiments in collaboration with teachers. In A. E. Kelly & R. A. Lesh (Eds.), *Handbook of research design in mathematics and science education* (pp. 307–333). Mahwah, NJ: Erlbaum.

Cobb, P., Yackel, E., & Wood, T. (1992). Interaction and learning in mathematics classroom situations. *Educational Studies in Mathematics, 23*(1), 99–122.

Collins, J., & Hansen, M. T. (2011). *Great by choice: Uncertainty, chaos, and luck—Why some thrive despite them all*. New York: HarperCollins.

Common Core State Standards Initiative. (2011). *Mathematics: Introduction: Standards for mathematical practice*. Accessed at www.corestandards.org/the-standards/mathematics /introduction/standards-for-mathematical-practice on November 15, 2011.

Confrey, J., Maloney, A. P., & Nguyen, K. (2010). *Learning trajectories display of the Common Core Standards for mathematics*. New York: Wireless Generation.

Conley, D. T., Drummond, K. V., de Gonzalez, A., Rooseboom, J., & Stout, O. (2011). *Reaching the goal: The applicability and importance of the Common Core State Standards to college and career readiness.* Eugene, OR: Educational Policy Improvement Center. Accessed at www .epiconline.org/files/pdf/ReachingtheGoal-FullReport.pdf on December 20, 2011.

Council of Chief State School Officers. (2008). *Educational leadership policy standards: ISLLC 2008 as adopted by the National Policy Board for Educational Administration.* Washington, DC: Author.

Danielson, C. (2009). *Talk about teaching! Leading professional conversations.* Thousand Oaks, CA: Corwin Press.

Darling-Hammond, L. (2010). *The flat world and education: How America's commitment to equity will determine our future.* New York: Teachers College Press.

Daro, P., McCallum, W., & Zimba, J. (2012, February 16). *The structure is the standards* [Web log post]. Accessed at http://commoncoretools.me/2012/02/16/the-structure-is-the -standards/ on March 11, 2012.

DuFour, R., DuFour, R., & Eaker, R. (2008). *Revisiting professional learning communities at work: New insights for improving schools.* Bloomington, IN: Solution Tree Press.

DuFour, R., DuFour, R., Eaker, R., & Many, T. (2010). *Learning by doing: A handbook for professional learning communities at work* (2nd ed.). Bloomington, IN: Solution Tree Press.

Dweck, C. (2006). *Mindset: The new psychology of success.* New York: Random House.

Easton, L. B. (Ed.). (2008). *Powerful designs for professional learning.* Oxford, OH: National Staff Developers Council.

Education Trust. (2005). *Gaining traction, gaining ground: How some high schools accelerate learning for struggling students.* Washington, DC: Author.

Equity. (2011). In *Merriam-Webster's online dictionary* (11th ed.). Accessed at www.merriam-webster .com/dictionary/equity on June 4, 2011.

Fernandez, C., & Yoshida, M. (2004). *Lesson study: A Japanese approach to improving mathematics teaching and learning.* Mahwah, NJ: Erlbaum.

Ferrini-Mundy, J., Graham, K., Johnson, L., & Mills, G. (Eds.). (1998). *Making change in mathematics education: Learning from the field.* Reston, VA: National Council of Teachers of Mathematics.

Fisher, D., Frey, N., & Rothenberg, C. (2011). *Implementing RTI with English learners.* Bloomington, IN: Solution Tree Press.

Fleischman, H. L., Hopstock, P. J., Pelczar, M. P., & Shelley, B. E. (2010). *Highlights from PISA 2009: Performance of U.S. 15-year-old students in reading, mathematics, and science literacy in an international context.* Washington DC: Institute of Education Sciences, National Center for Education Statistics.

Forman, E. (2003). A sociocultural approach to mathematics reform: Speaking, inscribing, and doing mathematics within communities of practice. In J. J. Kilpatrick, W. G. Martin, & D. Schifter (Eds.), *A research companion to principles and standards for school mathematics* (pp. 289–303). Reston, VA: National Council of Teachers of Mathematics.

Fullan, M. (2008). *The six secrets of change*. San Francisco: Jossey-Bass.

Fulton, K., & Britton, T. (2011). *STEM teachers in professional learning communities: From good teachers to great teaching*. Washington, DC: National Commission on Teaching and America's Future. Accessed at www.nctaf.org/wp-content/uploads/NCTAFreport STEMTeachersinPLCsFromGoodTeacherstoGreatTeaching.pdf on December 20, 2011.

Garmston, R., & Wellman, B. (2009). *The adaptive school: A sourcebook for developing collaborative groups*. Norwood, MA: Christopher-Gordon.

Ginsburg, H., & Dolan, A. (2011). Assessment. In F. Fennell (Ed.), *Achieving fluency: Special education and mathematics* (pp. 85–103). Reston, VA: National Council of Teachers of Mathematics.

Goleman, D. (2007). *Social intelligence: The new science of human relationships*. New York: Bantam Books.

Graham, P., & Ferriter, B. (2008). One step at a time. *Journal of Staff Development, 29*(3), 38–42.

Grover, R. (Ed.). (1996). *Collaboration: Lessons learned series*. Chicago: American Association of School Librarians.

Hattie, J. C. (2009). *Visible learning: A synthesis of over 800 meta-analyses relating to achievement*. New York: Routledge.

Haycock, K. (1998). *Good teaching matters . . . a lot*. Santa Cruz, CA: The Center for the Future of Teaching and Learning. Accessed at www.cftl.org/documents/K16.pdf on June 5, 2011.

Hiebert, J., Gallimore, R., Garnier, H., Bogard Givvin, K., Hollingsworth, H., Jacobs, J., et al. (2003). *Highlights from the 1999 TIMSS video study of eighth-grade mathematics teaching* (NCES 2003–011). Washington, DC: National Center for Education Statistics.

Hiebert, J., & Grouws, D. A. (2007). The effects of classroom mathematics teaching on students' learning. In F. K. Lester (Ed.), *Second handbook of research on mathematics teaching and learning*. Charlotte, NC: Information Age.

Hiebert, J., & Stigler, J. (1999). *The teaching gap: Best ideas from the world's teachers for improving education in the classroom*. New York: Free Press.

Horn, I. S. (2010). Teaching replays, teaching rehearsals, and re-visions of practice: Learning from colleagues in a mathematics teacher community. *Teachers College Record, 112*(1), 225–250.

Huggins, K. S., Scheurich, J. J., & Morgan, J. R. (2011). Professional learning communities as a leadership strategy to drive math success in an urban high school serving diverse, low-income students: A case study. *Journal of Education of Students Placed at Risk, 16*(2), 67–88.

Inside Mathematics. (2010). *Tools for principals & administrators*. Accessed at www.inside mathematics.org/index.php/tools-for-teachers/tools-for-principals-and-administrators on November 15, 2011.

Inside Mathematics. (2011). *Common Core standards for mathematical practice*. Accessed at http:// insidemathematics.org/index.php/common-core-standards on December 20, 2011.

Institute for Mathematics and Education. (2007). *Progressions documents for the Common Core math standards.* Accessed at http://ime.math.arizona.edu/progressions on November 15, 2011.

Johnson, E., Smith, L., & Harris, M. (2009). *How RTI works in secondary schools.* Thousand Oaks, CA: Corwin Press.

Kanold, T. (2011a). *The five disciplines of PLC leaders.* Bloomington, IN: Solution Tree Press.

Kanold, T. (2011b, April 18). Formative assessment in a summative assessment world. [Web log post]. Accessed at http://tkanold.blogspot.com/2011/04/formative-assessment-in-summative.html on December 20, 2011.

Kanold, T., Briars, D., & Fennell, F. (2012). *What principals need to know about teaching and learning mathematics.* Bloomington, IN: Solution Tree Press.

Kersaint, G. (2007). The learning environment: Its influence on what is learned. In W. G. Martin, M. E. Strutchens, & P. C. Elliot (Eds.), *The learning of mathematics: 69th yearbook* (pp. 83–96). Reston, VA: National Council of Teachers of Mathematics.

Knight, J. (2011). *Unmistakable impact: A partnership approach for dramatically improving instruction.* Thousand Oaks, CA: Corwin Press.

Kober, N., & Renter, D. S. (2011). *Common Core State Standards: Progress and challenges in school districts' implementation.* Washington, DC: Center on Educational Policy. Accessed at www.cep-dc.org/displayDocument.cfm?DocumentID=374 on December 19, 2011.

Kohn, A. (2011). Corridor wit: Talking back to our teachers. *Education Week, 31*(5), 28.

Larson, M. R. (2009). A curriculum decision-maker's perspective on conceptual and analytical frameworks for studying teachers' use of curriculum materials. In J. T. Remillard, B. A. Herbel-Eisenmann, & G. M. Lloyd (Eds.), *Mathematics teachers at work: Connecting curriculum materials and classroom instruction* (pp. 93–99). New York: Routledge.

Larson, M. R. (2011). *Administrator's guide: Interpreting the Common Core State Standards to improve mathematics education.* Reston, VA: National Council of Teachers of Mathematics.

Larson, M. R., Fennell, F., Adams, T. L., Dixon, J. K., Kobett, B. M., & Wray, J. A. (2012). *Common Core mathematics in a PLC at Work: Grades 3–5.* Bloomington, IN: Solution Tree Press.

Learning Forward. (2011). *Standards for professional learning.* Author. Accessed at www.learningforward.org/standards/standards.cfm on November 15, 2011.

Lewis, C. (2002). *Lesson study: A handbook of teacher-led instructional change.* Philadelphia: Research for Better Schools.

Loucks-Horsley, S., Love, N., Stiles, K. E., Mundry, S., & Hewson, P. W. (2003). *Designing professional development for teachers of science and mathematics.* Thousand Oaks, CA: Corwin Press.

Loveless, T. (2012). How well are American students learning? *The 2012 Brown Center Report on American Education, 3*(1), 1–36. Accessed at www.brookings.edu/~/media/Files/rc/reports/2012/0216_brown_education_loveless/0216_brown_education_loveless.pdf on April 11, 2012.

Maine West Mathematics Department. (n.d.). *Common Core math initiative.* Accessed at https://sites.google.com/a/maine207.org/mw-math-department/home/common-core on December 20, 2011.

Martin, T. (Ed.). (2007). *Mathematics teaching today: Improving practice, improving student learning.* Reston, VA: National Council of Teachers of Mathematics.

Marzano, R. (2003). *What works in schools.* Alexandria, VA: Association for Supervision and Curriculum Development.

Marzano, R. (2007). *The art and science of teaching.* Alexandria, VA: Association for Supervision and Curriculum Development.

Marzano, R., Pickering, D., & Heflebower, T. (2010). *The highly engaged classroom.* Bloomington, IN: Marzano Research Laboratory.

McCallum, B., Black, A., Umland, K., & Whitesides, E. (n.d.). [Common Core Mathematical Practices model]. *Tools for the Common Core standards.* Accessed at http://commoncoretools.files.wordpress.com/2011/03/practices.pdf on March 7, 2012.

Morris, A. K., & Hiebert, J. (2011). Creating shared instructional products: An alternative approach to improving teaching. *Educational Researcher, 40*(1), 5–14.

Morris, A. K., Hiebert, J., & Spitzer, S. M. (2009). Mathematical knowledge for teaching in planning and evaluating instruction: What can preservice teachers learn? *Journal for Research in Mathematics Education, 40,* 491–529.

National Association for the Education of Young Children. (2002). *Early childhood mathematics: Promoting good beginnings.* Accessed at www.naeyc.org/files/naeyc/file/positions/psmath.pdf on March 5, 2012.

National Board for Professional Teaching Standards. (2010). *National board certification for teachers: Mathematics standards for teachers of students ages 11–18+.* Arlington, VA: Author.

National Center for Response to Intervention. (n.d.). *Monitoring progress.* Accessed at www.rti4success.org on June 15, 2011.

National Council of Supervisors of Mathematics. (2007). *Improving student achievement by leading effective and collaborative teams of mathematics teachers.* Denver, CO: Author.

National Council of Supervisors of Mathematics. (2008a). *Improving student achievement by leading the pursuit of a vision for equity.* Denver, CO: Author.

National Council of Supervisors of Mathematics. (2008b). *The PRIME leadership framework: Principles and indicators for mathematics education leaders.* Bloomington, IN: Solution Tree Press.

National Council of Supervisors of Mathematics. (2011). *Improving student achievement in mathematics by systematically integrating effective technology.* Denver, CO: Author.

National Council of Teachers of Mathematics. (1980). *Agenda for action: Problem solving.* Accessed at www.nctm.org/standards/content.aspx?id=17279 on June 25, 2011.

National Council of Teachers of Mathematics. (1989). *Curriculum and evaluation standards for school mathematics.* Reston, VA: Author.

National Council of Teachers of Mathematics. (1991). *Professional standards for teaching mathematics*. Reston, VA: Author.

National Council of Teachers of Mathematics. (1995). *Assessment standards for school mathematics*. Reston, VA: Author.

National Council of Teachers of Mathematics. (2000). *Principles and standards for school mathematics*. Reston, VA: Author.

National Council of Teachers of Mathematics. (2006). *Curriculum focal points for prekindergarten through grade 8 mathematics: A quest for coherence*. Reston, VA: Author.

National Council of Teachers of Mathematics. (2008a). *Equity in mathematics education: A position of the National Council of Teachers of Mathematics*. Accessed at www.nctm.org/about/content.aspx?id=13490 on October 15, 2011.

National Council of Teachers of Mathematics. (2008b). *Intervention. A position of the National Council of Teachers of Mathematics*. Accessed at www.nctm.org/about/content.aspx?id=30506 on October 15, 2011.

National Council of Teachers of Mathematics. (2008c). *The role of technology in the teaching and learning of mathematics*. Accessed at www.nctm.org/uploadedFiles/About_NCTM/Position_Statements/Technology%20final.pdf on April 18, 2012.

National Council of Teachers of Mathematics. (2009). *Focus in high school mathematics: Reasoning and sense making*. Reston, VA: Author.

National Council of Teachers of Mathematics. (2010). *Making it happen: A guide to interpreting and implementing Common Core State Standards for mathematics*. Reston, VA: Author.

National Council of Teachers of Mathematics. (2011). *Discourse: Questioning*. Accessed at www.nctm.org/resources/content.aspx?id=6730&itemid=6730&linkidentifier=id&menu_id=598 on December 20, 2011.

National Governors Association Center for Best Practices & Council of Chief State School Officers. (2010). *Common core state standards for mathematics*. Washington, DC: Authors. Accessed at www.corestandards.org/assets/CCSSI_Math%20Standards.pdf on November 22, 2010.

National Mathematics Advisory Panel. (2008). *Foundations for success: The final report of the National Mathematics Advisory Panel*. Washington, DC: U.S. Department of Education.

National Research Council. (2001). *Adding it up: Helping children learn mathematics*. Washington, DC: National Academies Press.

National Research Council. (2005). *How students learn: History, mathematics, and science in the classroom*. (M. S. Donovan & J. D. Bransford, Eds.). Washington, DC: National Academies Press.

National Research Council. (2009). *Mathematics learning in early childhood: Paths toward excellence and equity*. Washington, DC: National Academies Press.

Partnership for Assessment of Readiness for College and Careers. (2011). *PARCC model content frameworks.* Accessed at www.parcconline.org/parcc-content-frameworks on December 20, 2011.

PBS Teachers. (n.d.). *Resource roundups.* Accessed at www.pbs.org/teachers/resourceroundups on November 15, 2011.

Penuel, W. R., Fishman, B. J., Yamaguchi, R., & Gallagher, L. P. (2007). What makes professional development effective? Strategies that foster curriculum implementation. *American Educational Research Journal, 44*(4), 921–958.

Peske, H. G., & Haycock, K. (2006). *Teaching inequality: How poor and minority students are shortchanged on teacher quality.* Washington, DC: Education Trust. Accessed at www.edtrust.org/sites/edtrust.org/files/publications/files/TQReportJune2006.pdf on July 21, 2011.

Pink, D. (2009). *Drive: The surprising truth about what motivates us.* New York: Riverhead.

Popham, J. (2008). *Transformative assessment.* Alexandria, VA: Association for Supervision and Curriculum Development.

Popham, J. (2011a). Formative assessment—A process and not a test. *Education Week, 30*(21), 35–37.

Popham, J. (2011b). *Transformative assessment in action: An inside look at applying the process.* Alexandria, VA: Association for Supervision and Curriculum Development.

Porter, A., McMaken, J., Hwang, J., & Yang, R. (2011). Common core standards: The new U.S. intended curriculum. *Educational Researcher, 40*(3), 103–116.

Rasmussen, C., Yackel, E., & King, K. (2003). Social and sociomathematical norms in the mathematics classroom. In H. L. Schoen & R. I. Charles (Eds.), *Teaching mathematics through problem solving: Grades 6–12* (pp. 143–154). Reston, VA: National Council of Teachers of Mathematics.

Raymond, A. (1997). Inconsistency between a beginning elementary school teacher's mathematics beliefs and teaching practice. *Journal for Research in Mathematics Education, 28*(5), 550–576.

Reeves, D. B. (2003). *High performance in high poverty schools: 90/90/90 and beyond.* Denver, CO: Center for Performance Assessment. Accessed at www.sjboces.org/nisl/high%20performance%2090%2090%2090%20and%20beyond.pdf on June 5, 2011.

Reeves, D. (2006). *The learning leader: How to focus school improvement for better results.* Alexandria, VA: Association for Supervision and Curriculum Development

Reeves, D. (2009). *Leading change in your school: How to conquer myths, built commitment, and get results.* Alexandria, VA: Association for Supervision and Curriculum Development.

Reeves, D. (2010). *Transforming professional development into student results.* Alexandria, VA: Association for Supervision and Curriculum Development.

Reeves, D. (2011a). *Elements of grading: A guide to effective practices.* Bloomington, IN: Solution Tree Press.

Reeves, D. (2011b). *Elements of grading: A guide to effective practice: Study guide.* Accessed at www
.solution-tree.com/media/pdf/study_guides/Elements_of_Grading.pdf on December
20, 2011.

Reys, R., Lindquist, M. M., Lambdin, D. V., & Smith, N. L. (2009). *Helping children learn
mathematics.* Hoboken, NJ: Wiley.

Saunders, W. M., Goldenberg, C. N., & Gallimore, R. (2009). Increasing achievement by
focusing grade-level teams on improving classroom learning: A prospective, quasi-
experimental study of Title I schools. *American Educational Research Journal, 46*(4),
1006–1033.

Schmidt, W. H., Cogan, L. S., Houang, R. T., & McKnight, C. C. (2011). Content coverage differences across districts/states: A persisting challenge for U.S. education policy. *American Journal of Education, 117*(3), 399–427.

Schmoker, M. (2005). Here and now: Improving teaching and learning. In R. DuFour, R. Eaker,
& R. DuFour (Eds.), *On common ground: The power of professional learning communities* (pp. xi–xvi). Bloomington, IN: Solution Tree Press.

School Improvement in Maryland. (2010). *Introduction to the classroom-focused improvement process (CFIP).* Accessed at http://mdk12.org/process/cfip on December 21, 2011.

Seeley, C. L. (2009). *Faster isn't smarter: Messages about math, teaching and learning in the 21st
century.* Sausalito, CA: Math Solutions.

Shuhua, A. (2004). *The middle path in math instruction: Solutions for improving math education.*
Lanham, MD: Scarecrow Education.

Shulman, L. (1986). Those who understand: Knowledge growth in teaching. *Educational
Researcher, 15*(2), 4–14.

Siegler, R. (2003). Implications of cognitive science research for mathematics education. In J.
J. Kilpatrick, W. G. Martin, & D. Schifter (Eds.), *A research companion to principles
and standards for school mathematics* (pp. 289–303). Reston, VA: National Council of
Teachers of Mathematics.

SMARTER Balanced Assessment Consortium. (n.d.). *Consortium governance.* Olympia, WA: State
of Washington Office of Superintendent of Public Instruction. Accessed at www.k12
.wa.us/SMARTER/Governance.aspx on December 20, 2011.

Smith, M. S., & Stein, M. K. (2011). *5 practices for orchestrating productive mathematics discussions.* Thousand Oaks, CA: Corwin Press.

Stacey, K. C., & Wiliam, D. (in press). Technology and assessment in mathematics. In M. A.
Clements, C. Keitel, A. J. Bishop, F. K. S. Leung, & J. Kilpatrick (Eds.), *Third international handbook of mathematics education.* Dordrecht, The Netherlands: Springer.

Standards Management System. (n.d.). *Math questioning strategies: The art of questioning in
mathematics.* Accessed at http://sms.sdcoe.net/SMS/mas/mathQuestionStrategy.asp
on December 20, 2011.

Stein, M. K., Remillard, J., & Smith, M. S. (2007). How curriculum influences student learning.
In F. K. Lester (Ed.), *Second handbook of research on mathematics teaching and learning*
(pp. 319–369). Charlotte, NC: Information Age.

Stein, M. K., Smith, M. S., Henningsen, M. A., & Silver, E. A. (2009). *Implementing standards-based mathematics instruction: A casebook for professional development* (2nd ed.). New York: Teachers College Press.

Stepanek, J., Appel, G., Leong, M., Managan, M., & Mitchell, M. (2007). *Leading lesson study.* Thousand Oaks, CA: Corwin Press.

Stiggins, R. (2007). Assessment for learning: An essential function of productive instruction. In D. B. Reeves (Ed.), *Ahead of the curve: The power of assessment to transform teaching and learning* (pp. 59–76). Bloomington, IN: Solution Tree Press.

Stiggins, R. J., Arter, J. A., Chappuis, J., & Chappuis, S. (2006). *Classroom assessment for student learning: Doing it right—using it well.* Princeton, NJ: Educational Testing Service.

Stigler, J., Gonzales, P., Kawanka, T., Knoll, S., & Serrano, A. (1999). *The TIMSS videotape classroom study: Methods and findings from an exploratory research project on eighth-grade mathematics instruction in Germany, Japan, and the United States (1995).* Washington, DC: National Center for Education Statistics.

Stigler, J. W., & Heibert, J. (1999). *The teaching gap: Best ideas from the world's teachers for improving education in the classroom.* New York: Free Press.

Stronge, J. H. (2007). *Qualities of effective teachers.* Alexandria, VA: Association for Supervision and Curriculum Development.

Tate, W. F., & Rousseau, C. (2007). Engineering change in mathematics education: Research policy and practice. In F. K. Lester (Ed.), *Second handbook of research on mathematics teaching and learning* (pp. 1209–1246). Reston, VA: National Council of Teachers of Mathematics.

U.S. Department of Education. (1983). *A nation at risk: The imperative for educational reform.* Accessed at http://www2.ed.gov/pubs/NatAtRisk/index.html on December 10, 2011.

Ushomirsky, N., & Hall, D. (2010). *Stuck schools: A framework for identifying schools where students need change—now!* Washington, DC: Education Trust. Accessed at www.edtrust.org/sites/edtrust.org/files/publications/files/StuckSchools.pdf on February 26, 2012.

Waters, T., Marzano, R., & McNulty B. (2003). *Balanced leadership: What 30 years of research tells us about the effect of leadership on student achievement.* Denver, CO: McREL.

Wayne, A. J., Kwang, S. Y., Zhu, P., Cronen, S., & Garet, M. S. (2008). Experimenting with teacher professional development: Motives and methods. *Educational Researcher, 37*(8), 469–479.

Webb, N. L. (1997). *Criteria for alignment of expectations and assessments in mathematics and science and education.* Washington, DC: Council of Chief State School Officers. Accessed at http://facstaff.wcer.wisc.edu/normw/WEBBMonograph6criteria.pdf on April 5, 2012.

Webb, N. L. (2002). *Depth of knowledge levels for four content areas.* Accessed at http://providenceschools.org/media/55488/depth%20of%20knowledge%20guide%20for%20all%20subject%20areas.pdf on April 18, 2012.

Wei, R. C., Darling-Hammond, L., Andree, A., Richardson, N., & Orphanos, S. (2009). *Professional learning in the learning profession: A status report on teacher development in the United States and abroad*. Dallas, TX: National Staff Development Council.

Wellman, B., & Lipton, L. (2004). *Data driven dialogue: A facilitator's guide to collaborative inquiry*. Arlington, MA: MiraVia.

Wiliam, D. (2007a). Content then process: Teacher learning communities in the service of formative assessment. In D. Reeves (Ed.), *Ahead of the curve: The power of assessment to transform teaching and learning* (pp. 183–205). Bloomington, IN: Solution Tree Press.

Wiliam, D. (2007b). Keeping learning on track: Classroom assessment and the regulation of learning. In F. K. Lester (Ed.), *Second handbook of research on mathematics teaching and learning* (pp. 1053–1098). Charlotte, NC: Information Age.

Wiliam, D. (2011). *Embedded formative assessment*. Bloomington, IN: Solution Tree Press.

Wiliam, D., Lee, C., Harrison, C., & Black, P. (2004). Teachers developing assessment for learning: Impact on student achievement. *Assessment in Education: Principles, Policy & Practice, 11*(1), 49–65.

Wiliam, D., & Thompson, M. (2008). Integrating assessment with instruction: What will it take to make it work? In C. A. Dwyer (Ed.), *The future of assessment: Shaping teaching and learning* (pp. 53–82). Mahwah, NJ: Erlbaum.

Wilkins, A., & Education Trust Staff. (2006). *Yes we can: Telling truths and dispelling myths about race and education in America*. Washington, DC: Education Trust. Accessed at http://diversity.ucf.edu/documents/resources/YesWeCan.pdf on June 5, 2011.

Wise, L., & Alt, M. (2005). *Assessing vertical alignment*. Alexandria, VA: Human Resources Research Organization.

Wormeli, R. (2006). *Fair isn't always equal*. Portland, ME: Stenhouse.

Zbiek, R. M. (2010). The influence of technology on secondary school students' mathematics learning. In J. Lobato & F. K. Lester (Eds.), *Teaching and learning mathematics: Translating research for secondary school teachers* (pp. 39–44). Reston, VA: National Council of Teachers of Mathematics.

Index

Other books in the *Common Core Mathematics in a PLC at Work*™ series (edited by Timothy D. Kanold):

Common Core Mathematics in a PLC at Work™, Grades K–2 by Matthew R. Larson, Francis (Skip) Fennell, Thomasenia Lott Adams, Juli K. Dixon, Beth McCord Kobett, and Jonathan A. Wray
BKF566

Common Core Mathematics in a PLC at Work™, Grades 3–5 by Matthew R. Larson, Francis (Skip) Fennell, Thomasenia Lott Adams, Juli K. Dixon, Beth McCord Kobett, and Jonathan A. Wray
BKF568

Common Core Mathematics in a PLC at Work™, Grades 6–8 by Diane J. Briars, Harold Asturias, David Foster, and Mardi A. Gale
BKF574

Common Core Mathematics in a PLC at Work™, High School by Gwendolyn Zimmermann, John A. Carter, Timothy D. Kanold, and Mona Toncheff
BKF561

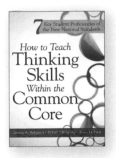
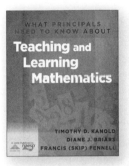
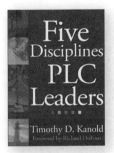

Solution Tree

Solution Tree's mission is to advance the work of our authors. By working with the best researchers and educators worldwide, we strive to be the premier provider of innovative publishing, in-demand events, and inspired professional development designed to transform education to ensure that all students learn.

The National Council of Teachers of Mathematics is a public voice of mathematics education, supporting teachers to ensure equitable mathematics learning of the highest quality for all students through vision, leadership, professional development, and research.